Last E

MW01282939

World War II Memories

D-Day to 70th Anniversary

By John Long & Walter Parks

Paperback Edition

Copyright 2014

UnKnownTruths

Publishing Company

UnKnownTruths

Publishing Company

8815 Conroy Windermere Rd. Ste 190

Orlando, FL 32835

UnknownTruths.com

info@UnknownTruths.com

Contents

Dedications

This book is dedicated to the men who served in World War II and more particularly, to the men who served in Operation Overlord (D-Day) and who were interviewed for this book to preserve their memories; lest we forget.

| Then | Now |

Oscar L. Russell was born November 1923 and enlisted in the US Navy in 1943 becoming a Gunner's Mate 2nd Class.

He was in the first wave of landing crafts to hit Omaha Beach at Pointe du Hoc on D-Day, June 6, 1944. Mr. Russell made it to the beach and stayed there for 28 days giving aid and removing bodies.

Among his various citations he was awarded the French Legion Medal of Honor and the Presidential Unit Citation.

After his military service, Russell stayed in the Navy Reserve, married and became a teacher and minister.

Out of 225 US Rangers; only 90 survived.

"I saw the US Rangers scaling the cliffs at Pointe du Hoc on Omaha Beach. You see, when they would stick their heads up they would shoot them. They would see their heads coming up and they were shooting those rangers off as they stuck their heads up...."

"I have been treated for the syndrome of memories coming back to me from the Battle of Normandy; young men in their prime; not only the landing, but living on the beach for 28 days. Handling the men and parts of men, and getting them on the hospital ships or sent to the grave yard."

"We had lost our ship.... We finally found a casualty ship, and made it back to England. While on the casualty ship, we had to remove wounded and dead from a smaller ship to a larger ship that took care of the wounded. What a horrible sight, seeing the dead and wounded; men missing parts of their bodies; parts of bodies just flopping over the side of the stretcher and the groans."

Oscar Russell

| Then | Now |

Bradford C. Freeman was born September 24, 1924 and enlisted December 12, 1942. He was assigned to Easy Company, 506th PIR, 101st Division which was depicted in Tom Hanks' movie *Band of Brothers*.

Mr. Freeman parachuted behind the enemy lines of Utah Beach at about 1:00 a.m. on June 6, 1944. He was later wounded and received the Purple Heart.

Mr. Freeman earned many medals: Bronze Star, Purple Heart with Oak Leaf, Europe Campaign with four Stars and one Arrowhead, WWII Victory, Army Occupation, Germany, French Croix de Guerre with Palm, 60 year WWII Anniversary, D-Day, Battle of the Bulge, Overseas Service, Combat Service, French Normandy, Defense of the Americans, French Liberation, Austria Liberation, Belgium Liberation, Dutch Cross, Victory in Europe, Army Good Conduct and the American Campaign.

After the war, Mr. Freeman worked for the United States Postal Service until retirement to his farm.

Tom Hanks and Bradford Freeman

"You trust them. You might not even know his name but he was a paratrooper and you are supposed to depend on him and you expected him to depend on you."

***

"They tell me that on D-Day I was in the first three planes. The field I landed in was several miles inland from the beach. There were five pretty white-faced cows, nobody else around. "

"We used crickets to signal for assemble."

Cricket

Bradford Freeman

Then	Now

William D. Fasking was born February 24, 1922 and enlisted June 6, 1940 in the Air Force and became a glider pilot.

He flew a Horsa glider with 13 troops and a trailer load of ammunition, landing south of St. Mere Eglise on D-Day.

Fasking was promoted to First Lieutenant on September 29, 1944. He served in Normandy, the Ardennes and in Central Europe. He participated in Operation Varsity, which was the last major airborne operation of World War II.

He was awarded many medals including the Air Medal with two Oak Clusters, European Theater Ribbon and the French Legion Medal of Honor.

After his military service Fasking owned and operated a service station until retirement.

"...Eventually, when we landed over there in Normandy, the Airborne Lieutenant was looking over my shoulder and the field I was supposed to go into and the one I had planned on; was only one glider in it....

There was one guy laying on the ground out there but there didn't seem to be anything else there, and I just started to turn in there and he said, "any place but there" so I just flipped her around to the right.

There was another little field there about 500 feet so I figured I could get it in there and knock the gear off.

After he told me that, instead of going and sitting down he.... To begin with, he told all the troops whatever you do sit in your seats. I told them. I told him. I told everybody. I kept repeating that stuff all the time. You are better off sitting in the seat and I will be damn he was still standing there when I kicked that thing sideways and tried to knock the gear off.

I got the one gear and didn't get the nose and it doubled back in there and the strut on it came up through the floor and hit him."

William D. Fasking

9

| Then | Now |

Earnest Bernard Wallace was born January 13, 1920 and enlisted in 1942 as a paratrooper and was assigned to Fox Company, 506th PIR 101st Airborne Division.

He jumped behind enemy lines shortly after 1:00 AM. June 6, 1944 and cut himself loose from his parachute at 1:20 AM.

He was injured twice. He received shrapnel wound while in Normandy and was hit in the face and chipped front tooth in Holland.

He was awarded the Purple Heart, 2 Bronze Stars and the French Legion Medal of Honor.

Mr. Wallace worked for the railroad 34 years until he retired.

"Well we jumped in Normandy, supposed to jump at 300 feet, but when they got to shooting at us, you know I couldn't wait to get there and I looked down and saw all them ships and I didn't know there were that many ships in the world.

In fact I didn't know what it was. I asked somebody what it was and they said that they are ships going in the English Channel to France, and so when we hit the coast I thought it was popcorn popping but it was bullets going through."

I could see and smell where the tracers went through that line of shooting. All I could see was tracers. …. when they got to shooting at us…. We jumped in Normandy at 300 feet altitude…. I cut my chute off at 1:20 AM D-Day morning and the beach invasion wasn't until 6:00 AM."

"Coming down out of the plane I could see the highway. It looked like water, but with all the equipment on me, and I couldn't collapse that chute, and I knew I was going to hit water and it frightened me pretty good, but I went under the power line beside the highway and my chute went over the power line, my head was in the ditch beside the highway, my feet was right towards the highway with my chute on top of me.

You talk about a mess. That was a mess. But somehow, I don't remember too much about how I got out, but I had a dagger strapped to my leg and I finally got my dagger out and I think I cut myself loose.

Finally I got up and I heard somebody coming down the highway and we had these little brown crickets and I clicked it and he answered me and it was my supply Sergeant"

Earnest Wallace

| Then | Now |

Harold F. Powers was born September 9, 1921 and drafted September 1942. He volunteered for paratroopers and was assigned to the 501st PIR 101st Airborne Division jumping early in the morning on D-Day.

Mr. Powers was captured later that day and was a POW until Germany surrendered about 11 months later.

He was awarded the French Legion Medal of Honor, World War II Victory Medal, European-Africa-Middle Eastern Campaign Medal, American Campaign Medal, Good Conduct Medal, Prisoner of War Medal, and two Bronze Stars.

Mr. Powers received a degree in Journalism and retired after a career in newspaper and advertising.

[Interviewed December 9, 2013; died 23 days later on January 1, 2014.]

"When I jumped I looked up and there was not a soul coming out of the other planes that came over and I knew something was wrong. We were all strung out. Only five of the 14 that jumped with me survived. The Germans shot some of us and captured the rest."

"When they asked us to surrender, he said they got us surrounded. We had no choice and when we stood up and I looked back over through the hedgerow they had guns right in the back of us and in front of us."

"After we got captured they took us to a place there on Normandy that we called Starvation Hill. We went without food for about a week.

They put us on the train and carried us up near Paris to talk to us and see what we knew and interrogate us. We wasn't giving them anything you know, no information, but they got us in groups that were captured together.

When they got me in there they wanted to know where we came from and all that sort of stuff you know, where did we fly out of and I said I don't know.

They questioned me some more about that. They said well who does know and I said ya'll killed him. I said you killed the one, our leader. They got disgusted with not knowing.

I said I am just a private, so they let me go and from there we went to Paris and caught a train out of there back into Germany to camps to get the dog tags that the prisoners got, and kept moving back until we got to an English prison camp.

We stayed there until September and they moved us out from there…. I ended up then in Czechoslovakia, in a coal mine area. I first started out digging out bomb shelters and then it got so cold we Americans couldn't take that so they let us go into the coal mines and took the Russians out to do that outside labor."

Harold Powers

| Then | Now |

Jack Carver was born May 19, 1923 and drafted in 1943. He was assigned as an Air Force flight engineer and flew in a C-47 aircraft that dropped paratroopers the night of D-Day.

He received many medals including Air Medal (plus two Bronze Clusters), Presidential Unit Citation, Euro-African-Middle Eastern Campaign Medal (with one silver star and two bronze), National Defense Service and French Legion Medal of Honor.

Mr. Carver made a career in the United States Air Force.

[Interviewed December 1, 2013; died 38 days later on January 8, 2014.]

Local Bank Honored Mr. Carver Just Before His Death

"You could see the black smoke starting, just popping out right all around our airplanes. …. the paratroopers jumped…. we turned to head back home…. there was a big explosion. I thought it was our airplane. I was scared to step back, scared I would fall through a hole. But it wasn't my airplane; it was the airplane flying on my right wing with both his engines on fire. We watched them hit the ground. They all got out alive."

Jack Carver

15

| Then | Now |

B. Eugene Meier was born January 6, 1921 and enlisted in May of 1942. He rose to the rank of First Lieutenant, serving with the 146th Combat Engineer Battalion that waded onto Omaha Beach at H Hour plus 3 minutes with 40 pounds of explosives on their backs to destroy obstacles on the beach.

He received a Purple Heart and the ETO Ribbon with five stars, Bronze Arrowhead for the invasion of Normandy, Bronze Star for Hurtgen Forest Battle, Army Presidential Unit Citation, Navy Presidential Unit Citation, World War II Victory Medal, Battle of the Bulge Commemorative Medal, D-Day Commemorative Medal, Combat Service Medal, French Medal of Liberation, Czechoslovakia Medal of Military Merit and the French Legion of Honor Medal.

After his service he was employed with Capital Airways until retirement.

[Interviewed October, 30, 2013; died 16 days later on November 16, 2013.]

"I was the officer in charge. I had 23 enlisted men and a combat medic in my landing craft, an LCM. When we loaded, we sailed on the Princess Maud, which was a coastal steamer, channel steamer, and it anchored off the shore.

We loaded on the 5th and unloaded that night. We unloaded because of the storm and we loaded up again the night of the 5th and sailed.

I and each one of the enlisted men carried a canvas sack on our chest holding eight 2.5 lb blocks of plastic explosives. We had another pack of this, identical pack on our back so each one of us carried 40 lbs. of explosives, 20 on our chest and 20 on our back, along with other special equipment that we were carrying, such as detonators."

***

"On Christmas morning, we had the most severe, coldest and heaviest snow fall in the weather history in Germany and Europe at that year. We were in the middle of an artillery bombardment when our chaplain drove up. He was visiting all the front lines that he could find, so he pulled in and used the hood of his jeep as an altar and, kneeling, he read mass for us. We lay on the ground because of this heavy artillery bombardment.

I can never say enough for the most ignored group of men in the military and that is your chaplains."

Eugene Meier

| Then | Now |

Ivy C. Agee was born April 3, 1923 and drafted January 10, 1943. He served in the 111th Field Artillery Battalion, 116th Infantry Regiment, 29th Infantry Division, Battery B during the D-Day invasion.

His battles and campaigns include Operation Overlord, D-Day Normandy invasion, Northern France, Ardennes, Rhineland, and Central Europe

He received several medals including the Silver Star, Bronze Star, European African Mideast Campaign Arrow head with 4 Bronze Stars, World War II Victory Medal, Army Presidential Unit Citation, French Croix de Guerre with Palm and French Legion of Honor Medal.

After his military service Mr. Agee returned to his family's dairy farm until retirement.

"I was in the first wave of the invasion; bodies were flying everywhere. There was blood on the edge of the water; the beach was just running with pure blood."

"Almost all of the soldiers in the first assault wave on the beaches were killed."

I had to crawl across two dead soldiers to get behind some protection.... I crawled from shell hole to shell hole and I finally got to where I could relax and not be afraid of being captured or being blown up."

"When we got off the beach, we had a wonderful success because we got to where the Germans had left this sand table that they made all their gun positions in. They had to leave so fast they didn't destroy the sand table and the sand table showed us where their guns were. That was a great advantage that we could see where their guns were and destroy them."

Ivy Agee

| Then | Now |

James L. Springer was born January 21, 1920 and drafted January 16, 1943. Springer was a Staff Sergeant in the 38th Regiment, 2nd Infantry Division.

He was wounded twice and received two Purple Hearts. On June 12th he was shot by a sniper in the right ear and the bullet scraped his scalp. He was able to return to duty and was promoted on July 9th.

He was wounded again on September 7, 1944 by shrapnel in the chest and arm from German artillery. He was unable to return to combat after that injury and was discharged from the Army in March of 1945.

He was awarded several medals including 2 Purple Hearts, 2 Bronze Star and French Legion Medal of Honor.

After his military service Mr. Springer worked in corporate management in planning and production.

"On D-Day the sky was just black with airplanes going over. It was quite a sight. On D-Day plus 1 we climbed down a rope from the ship to the landing craft and we went close to France on Omaha Beach and got off the landing craft. Water was about chest deep. We got on the beach; I think we stayed on the beach overnight. The next day we marched into France and started the combat."

"I was with a squadron sent to hunt snipers. We knew there were a bunch of Germans up there in that next area and I was placing my men along the hedgerow and I told one guy to get down and as soon as he got down the sniper fire got him. It came out the back of his head, brains and everything pouring out the back of his head. I still feel I was responsible."

"In my first injury I got shot in the ear, it went through my ear and out the back. Extremely lucky, an inch to the left could have been it. I was in the hospital for six weeks."

"I got my second injury somewhere outside of Brest. Mortars were shelling in air.

We had the first hot meal we had had and they was serving it when the shells started bursting in air. Shrapnel went through my chest and into my lung and broke my arm. The shrapnel came from air bursts."

"The medic came and got me on a stretcher and was taking me down to the first aid station. He said that the hole was too big and I was losing too much blood, I am going to have to sew it up, so he put me down on the ground and sewed up that hole and took me on to the field hospital.

I don't know whether it was that day or some other day later they operated on me in the field hospital; German captives or orderlies were at the hospital."

James L. Springer

Then	Now

Lawrence "Rabbit" Kennedy was born July 5, 1922 and enlisted October 9, 1940. He was assigned to the 83rd Field Artillery, 2nd Battalion, 8th Battery, 71st Artillery Armored Division that joined the combat in Normandy six days after the invasion.

In addition to World War II he also served in the Korean conflict and Vietnam.

After a 35 year long military career he retired to his home near Amory, Mississippi, as Command Sergeant Major. He is one of the highest decorated veterans in the armed forces. A room in the Amory Museum is devoted to him.

"When D-Day came my outfit did not go on D-Day landing. We had to trade those 2-1/2 ton trucks in for a big heavy weight artillery self-propelled artillery and they had to wait until the infantry cleared the beaches so we could go ashore in them heavy, heavy artillery pieces.

That was six days after D-Day when we landed in Normandy. The bodies were still floating out in the water that Germany had sank the LSTs, dead soldiers were everywhere.

The only thing that kept them floating was the heavy packs they had on them, used really to help the guy to stay without drowning, but the Germans kept shooting and killing everybody. Them packs just kept the bodies from going down."

"We walked across France and fought for what seemed like forever and every day they would haul out dead people, frozen in their foxholes."

"I became a grown man overnight."

***

"Let me say a word about Vietnam. Me and my commanding General would go visit the wounded at the hospital every Sunday. There were two guys there. I will never forget it.

One said Sergeant Major, call my wife, and he was crying. We could use telephone conversations in Vietnam that we didn't have in World War II. I couldn't hold it no longer, I broke down…the general saw me crying and put his arm around my shoulder and I said to him I must be weak, I can't stop from crying, and he said "Sergeant Major, cry all you want to, I wouldn't let my daughter marry a man who wouldn't cry."

Rabbit Kennedy

| Then | Now |

Olin Baxter McKee was born June 20, 1923 and drafted January 23, 1943. He was assigned to Battery B, 266th Field Artillery Battalion. Mr. McKee was the youngest man in his company and rose to the rank of First Sergeant He moved heavy artillery onto Omaha Beach 20 days after D-Day.

He served in 5 campaigns: Normandy, Northern France, Ardennes, Rhineland and Central Europe and received the EAMET Theater Campaign Medal with five Bronze Service Stars and American Theater Campaign Medal.

After his military service Mr. McKee owned and operated his own business.

"One day, I was with the captain going out to find a suitable fire place. You couldn't just put those guns up anywhere.

We located an area that we thought would be a good area for our gun and the captain told me to stay there with the driver and the radio operator and he went on with another company to help them find a location.

I was kind of nosy. We were parked on a high embankment, probably 15 foot high, and the infantry had had a pretty good battle in that area. There was a pasture over here and a pretty good patch of woods and I was sitting there in the car just waiting on time and decided to get out and I got out and climbed up that embankment and looking down in the woods there was a body that had on American camouflage.

I assumed it was an American. I kept watching and all of a sudden he blinked and so I got back to the car and called the captain and they came back there.

It ended up we got three Germans out of that patch of woods that had been in combat the day before. We got them started back to the compound and one of them reached in his pocket and pulled out a hand grenade.

He had been searched by four or five people. How he hid that grenade we will never know. He pulled it out and threw it out but didn't pull the trigger on it, just threw it away because he got too close and he knew if he went into the American compound with that he would get killed.

That was one of the biggest scares I had when I saw this fellow."

"I think it [the war] made a better man out of me; more responsibility and made me grow up."

HIS Sister (Christine Smith): Olin has never failed to fly the American flag. The flag has been a part of his life, as in all of ours, but particularly him. He is proud of that flag.

Olin McKee

Joseph Ruben Johnson was born May 31, 1925, enlisted October 14, 1943, served in Battery D, 551st AAA Antiaircraft Automatic Weapons Battalion.

He was in the Normandy invasion, continued through Germany, blew up crematoriums at Dachau, and drove a jeep across Europe transporting arrested SS troops.

He received four Bronze Stars and was awarded the French Legion Medal of Honor.

After his service years Mr. Johnson owned and operated his private plumbing company.

"I want to tell the American people who the heroes were; they were the women in America, the United States women that lived in America in 1941 until 1945. They went to the shipyards and the airplane factories and ammunition factories and built all our war machines and sent it to us.

They were the greatest generation of women this world will ever know. Most of the women had a brother, father or husband in the war somewhere. They were both mother and father and they took care of the home front. Them women would go work eight hours in a defense factory.

This world don't know what a great blessing and sacrifice the American women sacrificed for World War II. They are the heroes. When we lost a tank they had three ready to go right up in the front. We never ran out of anything."

***

"The 551st AAA Antiaircraft Battalion that I was assigned to; we was assigned to guard the Second Armored Division, the Hell on Wheels and the 20th Co-Artillery. The Second Armored Division was one of the best armored divisions in the world and our job was to protect them from the air. They were supposed to protect us on the ground and we would protect them from the air."

"I was a driver, mostly jeep driver. I drove for Colonel Smith, a full eagle colonel, which was the aid to General Patton."

"I also worked with the CIA, driving all over Europe picking up arrested SS troops and transporting them to Nuremberg where the war trials were held."

Joe Johnson

| Then | Now |

George Pulakos was born in December 1922 and enlisted June 6, 1942 and became a surgical technician. He landed on Omaha Beach on D-Day and served as a medic. Later he was saving a wounded soldier when he was hit by shrapnel and lost part of his hand.

After extensive surgery and rehabilitation he received a medical discharge in 1945. He received the Purple Heart, Bronze Star and French Legion Medal of Honor.

After convalescence and discharge from the service Mr. Pulakos continued to work in the surgical supply field until his retirement in 1987.

"We were on the United States landing craft run by the Coast Guard. The medics were loaded in the back of the landing craft so the troops would go out first and we would follow and pick up the wounded so to speak.

We got hung up on this ship and a British landing craft came and went nose to nose and we reloaded onto that. Now, instead of being at the back of it I was in the front. I remember one fellow with me that was in the medic unit, he was 6 foot 2 or 3. The landing craft came to a crunch and dropped the front end of it down, he stepped off and he went into water up to his nose."

"I knew if I stepped off it was going to be well over my head, so I grabbed the chain and swung around and scampered to the back of it. I wasn't going to step off."

"They kept me on the beach, I could swim. I was a swimmer and I would recover bodies. We were stacking them like cord wood on the beach."

"For years I've carried horrific images in my head of all the bodies on the beach. They were stacked like cord wood, 4 and 5 feet high."

George Pulakos

Then   Now

Percy Scarborough was born May 22, 1925 and drafted September 1943. He was attached to H Company, 358th Infantry Regiment, 90th Division. Mr. Scarborough served primarily as a forward observer in a mortar unit.

Campaigns: Normandy, Northern France, Ardennes-Alsace, Rhineland, Central Europe. Mr. Scarborough was awarded the Bronze Star and he was also on the Honor Flight to Washington D.C. in October 2013.

After his military service he had a successful career in private business.

[Interviewed November 22, 2013; died 25 days later on December 17, 2013.]

"On D-Day the shelling was so bad that some LSTs didn't go all the way to the beach but dropped the solders off in too deep water and headed back. Some soldiers drowned and many lost their equipment. As quick as I could take cover I took cover and I stayed in cover practically all day of the invasion."

"One time when it was my turn as forward observer, I was sick and my buddy went up for me. About twenty minutes later I woke up and my buddy had been killed."

"We never need to go into another war. They should get out of all these messes overseas, leave it to them. They don't like us, they don't care anything about us and we are blowing our whole assets over there."

"War is waste; waste of finances, waste of human life; waste of everything. There is nothing ever good that comes out of war."

Percy Scarborough

"I hate war as only a soldier who has lived it can, only as one who has seen its brutality, its futility, its stupidity." **General Dwight D. Eisenhower (January 10, 1946)**

Special Thanks & Acknowledgements

This book would not have been possible without the help of many special people, especially the truly great men and their families who took time and opened their homes to tell us their stories. I have truly been blessed by your hospitality and count it as an honor to call you friends.

My wife Helen and I saw a documentary about the village of Graignes France. That motivated us to go to Normandy for the D-Day celebrations in 2013.

We would like to thank Dennis Small, Lord Mayor of Graignes for his assistance. He located two French women, Germaine Mahier and Marthe Rigault who gave us such a warm welcome and great eyewitness insights while we were in their village.

Before we left for Normandy, we talked with veteran Oscar Russell and his wife Helen about his D-Day experiences; and because of their encouragement and support we worked hard to put this book together.

We give special thanks to Lisa ("Punkin") Murphree who helped with the interviews and worked so hard in editing this book.

I must give special thanks to my wife Helen who helped me so very much with everything and especially with the interviews.

Helen and I want to thank all of those who helped us along the way, but most of all we thank the fourteen eyewitnesses and their families.

Introduction

"If ever proof were needed that we fought for a cause and not for conquest it could be found in these cemeteries. Here was our only conquest: all we ask… was enough… soil in which to bury our gallant dead." **General Mark W. Clark, 1969-1984, American Cemetery, Normandy**

This book was written to preserve the last personal voices of the truly great soldiers that went ashore at Normandy on June 6, 1944 or shortly thereafter.

Soon, all these brave men will pass to another time and place. We believe that these men should never be forgotten. Their personal memories must be preserved.

Their actions at this time in our history were clearly for a just cause. All of these soldiers that I interviewed knew that they were putting their lives at risk. They were highly motivated and well trained for the great tasks given them.

Paratroopers, glider pilots, artillery men, medics, dog soldiers, and even a sailor who witnessed Rangers storming the cliffs at Pointe du Hoc were personally interviewed.

The Interviewees ranged in age from 88 to 93 and to a man, each had some profound stories to tell.

Those landing on the beaches have burning memories of the great armada of ships and vessels in the avenging invasion of Normandy.

They remember the carnage of bodies on the beaches.

I asked one of our Interviewees, George Pulakos to describe his experiences on the beach.

GEORGE PULAKOS: They kept me on the beach, I could swim. I was a swimmer and I would recover bodies. We were stacking them like cord wood on the beach.

For years I've carried horrific images in my head of all the bodies on the beach. They were stacked like cord wood, 4 and 5 feet high.

We interviewed 14 of these warriors and this book may be the last documented eyewitness's memories of the D-Day invasion. Four have already died since our interviews of just a few months ago.

We interviewed Eugene Meier October 30, 2013; he died 17 days later on November 16, 2013 at age 90.

We interviewed Percy Scarborough November 22, 2013; he died 25 days later on December 17, 2013 at age 88.

We interviewed Jack Carver December 1, 2013; he died 38 days later on January 8, 2014 at age 90.

We interviewed Harold Powers December 9, 2013; he died 23 days later on January 1, 2014 at age 92.

This book is indeed about the last eyewitnesses' memories.

We begin this heroic, terrible, terrible war story in 1939. That was when the European war really started. That is when Germany invaded Poland, and Britain and France declared war on Germany.

Many books have been written about World War II, but most have concentrated on well known leaders and celebrated heroes. We wanted to tell the story through the eyes and memories of the common soldier.

Most of our heroic Interviewees had clear memories of the significant events they encountered.

We present their memories in their own words because we want you to be able to sense their emotions, their struggles to recall and find words to describe their memories and perhaps their states of frail health.

Being able to read their own words will hopefully help you to detect their enthusiasm for this project to preserve their memories.

The interviews are split into sections so that we can integrate their memories with the chronological and historical framework of their experiences.

We must confess that, at times in the interviews, we got a bit emotional. The interviews were so very visual that we could see the bodies floating in the waters at the beaches.

We could see our soldiers falling in the hedgerows and roads of the country side.

We could see our soldiers when they were captured and marched long distances in severe weather.

We could almost hear the gunfire and smell the gunpowder.

We could see the horrors of the German concentration camps.

Hopefully you will experience these same emotions as you read this book.

Chapter 1
Hitler Begins World War II

The world stood by as Hitler forced the union of Austria with Germany. He then occupied the Sudetenland and invaded Czechoslovakia as the world just continued to watch.

But when Hitler invaded Poland on September 1, 1939, Britain and France knew that they would be next. They had to act. They declared war on Germany two days later.

The USA would not declare war; we proclaimed our neutrality. The USA did, however begin to supply Britain with essential supplies.

This initiated the critical Battle of the Atlantic between German U-Boats and British naval convoys.

Most countries of the rest of Europe continued to wait without taking any action.

But some, including most of Scandinavia were becoming frightened.

The Soviet Union signed the Ribbentrop Pact with Germany in late August which resulted in Russia following Germany into Poland in September. They carved up Poland between the two of them before the end of the year.

Demarcation line: Poland
~ 28 Sept 1939 (—)

Russia then continued their aggression and invaded Finland. The Finnish Army inflicted severe damage on the Russians, but Russia persisted and defeated Finland in March of 1940.

Germany invaded Denmark and Norway in April.

Denmark surrendered immediately, but the Norwegians fought on with some assistance from the British and French.

On May 10, 1940, the same day Winston Churchill became Prime Minister of Britain, Germany invaded France, Belgium and Holland with their Blitzkrieg, known as the 'lightning war'.

Germany's Blitzkrieg was a combination of fast armored tanks on land and superiority in the air. It could not be stopped even with the help of British and French troops.

Holland and Belgium fell by the end of May; Paris was taken two weeks later.

Norway saw they would be fighting alone and therefore surrendered in June.

From May 27 to June 4, 1940 British and French troops retreated from the invaders in haste, and about 226,000 British and 110,000 French troops were rescued from the channel port of Dunkirk by a ragged fleet consisting of pleasure boats and Navy destroyers.

William Fasking Interview

This is when our first Interviewee Hero William Fasking joined the Army.

It was June 6, 1940, exactly four years before D-Day. William wanted to become a pilot. He later piloted a glider in the D-Day invasion.

I asked him why he joined before we got involved in the war.

WILLIAM FASKING: When I graduated from high school I told the old man that we are going to have to make some sort of arrangement because I am not going to work my butt off here for nothing like I have been doing, and he said, well dammit you are getting fed aren't you? I said well that is not enough and he said well by-god you can hit the road and I did. I started out walking.

I thought that I would just as well join the Army. In high school I did extra work for photography and I learned to develop pictures and enlarge them.

JOHN LONG: So you did graduate from high school?

WILLIAM FASKING: Yes, sir.

JOHN LONG: So you joined or did you get drafted?

WILLIAM FASKING: I joined. They didn't have the draft yet.

JOHN LONG: You were in there from the get-go.

WILLIAM FASKING: There wasn't any war going on, not with us. What I wanted was photography and it was full of course, and the next closest thing I could get into was radio. I worked my tail off on that.

I had gone through basic. I had learned most of the radios that we used. We used a 224B receiver. They had the 409 transmitter and they had another one, the 207 I think, anyway the 209 was used mostly in artillery and everything else, in the tanks, so I learned code.

JOHN LONG: Was there any particular reason why you joined that particular branch of service?

WILLIAM FASKING: Well yeah, it was Army, but it was Army-Air Force back then.

I first tried to get in one of the Academies, but they were full so I went ahead and joined the service.

JOHN LONG: Well after you got through the basic and the training with the radios; tell me how you went from there into the glider service.

WILLIAM FASKING: Well I finally graduated as a radio operator and they sent me to California in a training committee. All of California and Arizona was all cadets training.

Of course I applied for pilot training but there was no chance of getting in at the time. That's the reason I joined the glider program.

They didn't have gliders yet so we trained in bi-plane cubs. We learned to fly airplanes in Hose New Mexico and then we graduated and went to 29 Palms and started flying sail planes.

They gave us an hour of flight. They towed us up there and we caught the wind and had to return it in an hour. You couldn't stay up any longer than that.

After we graduated from that we went from 29 Palms to Albuquerque and they didn't have the cargo fliers ready yet either so they gave us the power planes to fly to get our flying time in and when they finally got the gliders in, they got some CB4As and we flew them until they figured we were good enough to graduate.

As a matter of fact sometimes you get a little head wind coming in to land, you could put that ole nose up, nose high slip and just almost come down like an elevator and straighten her out and go ahead and land.

JOHN LONG: So you finally achieved your goal of being up in the air at least? Do you recall, and give me just your best recollection, on making the transition from your training and then going overseas to England and that training.

WILLIAM FASKING: After that we went to Barefield Indiana at Ft. Wayne Indiana. We were not there very long and then we went up to; there were two places in New York where we got a ship out.

JOHN LONG: So you went over on a ship?

WILLIAM FASKING: Yeah, we went across on a ship; we went on the Mauretania, the sister ship to the Lusitania that got sunk early, the Germans sunk it.

JOHN LONG: You arrived in England about when?

WILLIAM FASKING: We went clear up in the North Sea because of the submarines. I was more worried about hitting an iceberg. They had the subs pretty well cleaned out by the time we went overseas, and that was in March, I think, 1942.

JOHN LONG: That meant then that you were in England a year and a half before the invasion?

WILLIAM FASKING: A lot of training, in the English gliders, the big horsies.

JOHN LONG: Tell us about the difference between the glider that you trained on and the one that you wound up having to fly when you got to England.

WILLIAM FASKING: Well, ours were metal; the CB4A was made out of metal framework and then covered over with plastic, the sides and stuff. I am trying to think of the material.

JOHN LONG: Was it wood, plywood?

WILLIAM FASKING: No, the only plywood in it was the floor and it was reinforced to carry jeeps and artillery pieces and the wood that's the main spar out there to support the wings and they had a strut down from the wing back down to the body of the glider but the rest of it was all metal framework and the canvas.

JOHN LONG: What I was trying to get at, in the back of my mind was, when you got to England and you were forced to use a different type glider you kind of had to get used to that type glider.

WILLIAM FASKING: Well yeah. That was the Horsa glider that I flew into Normandy. That was an English glider. I got a lot of time to test that.

English Horsa Glider

45

***

I'll get back to my interview with William Fasking a little later, but first we need to understand what was happening in the war shortly after he enlisted on June 6, 1940.

In July 1940 Hitler made a pact with the French hero of World War I, Marshall Petain, to form the French Vichy Government in North France and sign an armistice with Germany.

Marshall Petain

The Vichy Government later effectively became a puppet government to Germany.

This armistice lasted until November 1942, when the Germans took over all of France.

At the time, Charles de Gaulle, as the leader of the Free French, fled to England to continue the fight against Hitler.

Charles de Gaulle

After "handling" France, Hitler turned his attention to Britain and began preparations for an invasion.

The Battle of Britain was from July to September 1940 and was the first battle ever to be fought entirely in the air.

Britain had radar which helped it to achieve victory in the air battle, and therefore maintain air superiority. Without air superiority Germany had to postpone its invasion plans.

Everybody was talking about the air battle. Our Interviewee Hero Lawrence "Rabbit" Kennedy thought this would be a good time to join the Army. He joined October 9, 1940.

Lawrence "Rabbit" Kennedy Interview

Rabbit Kennedy was assigned to heavy artillery and took the first heavy artillery across the beaches when they were cleared 6 days after D-Day.

I asked him why he joined the Army so early.

RABBIT KENNEDY: We were destitute and poor. I decided I had to do something to survive. I left home, barefooted, and walked to Tupelo, Mississippi, October 9, 1940. I joined the Army, but I was four pounds light of the minimum weight limit so the recruiter told me to go across the street from the railroad station where the recruiting office was and eat me a dozen bananas and drink all the artisan water I could.

I got my bananas and I sat down in the railroad station and started eating bananas, and since then I have not eaten another banana.

I ate a dozen of them bananas. The recruiter was drinking that 180 proof alcohol that they sold there and he didn't even weigh me, he told me I was alright.

So we left there and they sent me to Ft. Benning Georgia and I was assigned to a horse outfit that pulled French 75 Howitzers. I thought when I left home I would never have to worry about a mule or a horse nowhere, but I wound up in a horse outfit.

My outfit left there and went to Ft. Jackson South Carolina and we trained in horse drawn artillery pieces out in the woods near Camden South Carolina. Then the Army sent us to Fort Sill Oklahoma, the artillery base; we went there and we were trained on artillery pieces out in the open range at Ft. Sill.

On December 7, 1941, when the Japanese attacked Pearl Harbor they took all their horses down to the stable and started shipping them in a cable car down to Fort Riley Kansas and we started to get in Dodge 2-1/2 ton trucks to fill those Howitzers with.

Then sometime in 1942 we went to Indiantown Gap Pennsylvania preparing to go to England, in preparation for D-Day.

***

We'll return to Rabbit Kennedy later. Let's first get back to the chronological events of the war.

Even though Hitler had loss the air battle with Britain and postponed his plan to invade Britain, he continued his 'Blitz' of Britain's cities. Their 'Blitz' resulted in the loss of about 40,000 civilian lives.

The combination of all of these events convinced many in the US that it was just a matter of time before we would enter the war.

At the time our Army was divided into three parts: the regulars numbered 243,095, the National Guard was 226,837 and the Organized Reserve numbered 104,228.

It was clear that we needed to start preparing.

On June 17, 1941 the Army was expanded to 280,000 men; and nine days later to 375,000.

Roosevelt persuaded Congress to pass the Selective Service Act and by July 606,915 men were inducted into the Army.

Meanwhile Hitler studied Napoleon's disastrous invasion of Russia, but so coveted Russia that he invaded anyway. He invaded Russia on June 22, 1941.

This was Hitler's biggest mistake of the war.

Stalin ordered his troops to retreat and leave a "burned earth" for the Germans.

Germany's initial advance was swift. Hitler's army seemed to be progressing as well in Russia as they had earlier in

49

Western Europe. Sebastopol fell at the end of October, in only about 4 months.

Hitler then moved on and attacked Moscow at the end of the year.

The bitter Russian winter, however, like the one that Napoleon had experienced a century and a half earlier, crippled the Germans.

In December 1941 Hitler's troops had advanced to within 20 miles of Moscow. Stalin was ready to reverse his fall back tactics. The Soviets counterattacked on December 5 and pushed Hitler back about 50 miles from Moscow.

This was Hitler's first significant defeat of the war.

Chapter 2
Pearl Harbor, US Enters the War

December 7, 1941, a day that President Roosevelt said would live in infamy; the Japanese mounted a surprise attacked on the US base at Pearl Harbor in Hawaii.

This was Japan's biggest mistake of the war.

The US declared war on Japan.

A few days later Germany declared war on the US. Winston Churchill was delighted because it meant the US would actively participate with England in the war.

The US was now firmly in the war. Six of our 14 Interviewee Heroes followed the two who had previously joined in 1940 and joined in 1942.

Oscar Russell Interview

Oscar L. Russell enlisted in the Navy in 1942 shortly after Pearl Harbor.

I asked him why he decided to go into the Navy rather than the Army.

OSCAR RUSSELL: One of my cousins was walking down the street and I asked him what he was doing, and he said the Japanese had declared war on the United States and he was going to sign up for it, and that's when I got in.

Then I went to Camp Shelby and they were going to put me in the Army and I told them no I didn't want in the Army, that I had signed up for the Navy and that's where I wanted to go, so they put me over in the Navy then. I got in the Navy and then I went up to Bainbridge Maryland and took my boot training.

Then I went to Washington DC; I think this is about the time Mussolini went into Africa.

JOHN LONG: Yeah, Mussolini envisioned himself the leader of a revived Roman Empire. He felt Rome was destined to rule the world, again.

He invaded Ethiopia because it was one of two African states, the other being Liberia, not already colonized by any European nation and it was the closer of the two for the Italians and it was flanked by the other Italian-controlled countries of Eritrea and Italian Somaliland.

He also perceived Ethiopia as militarily weak.

OSCAR RUSSELL: Well I didn't know all of that. Anyway, we went down to Washington DC to train and experiment with French mustard and Lucite gas. They knew that the Germans had started using that.

They gave us special gear where we would be covered all up with all this special type of water proof and gas proof clothes. Now, they put us in this gas chamber and it was just like a Quonset hut, so they put us in there and at first they just give us a little tear gas and let us work with the tear gas, and then we had to go in and they used the Lucite gas and the French mustard gas, and they even put washers on our hands and put the liquid gas in those washers and they would make big blisters on the fellows where they put those on, it would make big blisters on them, so we had to go through that.

I was one of about 4000 in that training.

JOHN LONG: Did they tell you why you were taking this type of training?

OSCAR RUSSELL: Yeah. For the GI's for the invasion.

JOHN LONG: Where did you go to catch the ship headed to England?

OSCAR RUSSELL: I went and got on the, uh I don't remember the name, but I remember that there was a submarine out there. They went a way up north because it was a submarine and they could out run a submarine so they could get on that big ship, and they said that was the further north then they had ever been, but they could out run that submarine and go up that way.

I believe then they went over to Liverpool, I believe it was Liverpool where I got off the ship, and then they had to transfer us to another place, and they put us on these little ole train cars.

JOHN LONG: Then where did you go from Liverpool?

OSCAR RUSSELL: We had to make a long trip up through there. I think we went to Scotland, I believe. We saw those fellows with skirts on. We thought it was funny to see men with skirts on.

They put us in this little Quonset hut thing, and some of the officers would make the men, in that cold weather get out and line up and stand up and wait, you know how you had to do every morning; well our skipper told us that men, there is no use in us going out there and standing up in that cold.

He said I will give you five minutes, and when I tell you to get out there you get out there, so we got out there in ship shape in just that short time. Then they would take us marching way up there in, there was snow all up in the mountains there and he would tell us, now men, I don't see any sense in all this marching here, you are Navy men.

He would tell us we could go up there and play, and throw snow balls at each other, but he said when we get down to that gate you better be ship shape, and we did it pretty good, but you know there is always one fellow that goofs off and this one fellow he goofed off.

He said I told y'all; and boy he took us back up in those hills, then he brought us back to the gate, and man, he made us march and come in that gate, march and come in that gate, march and come in that gate, and when we got through with that other fellow he never did mess up no more.

He was in step. So we waited that long time and he took us that day on that ship, it was around 8000 or something like that.

JOHN LONG: Did you take a train to get there?

OSCAR RUSSELL: Oh yeah, we took one of those little trains, I think we went back to, I think it was Portsmouth or

Plymouth in the lower end of England to get ready to go for the invasion. We were a mess up in there.

***

I'll provide the early part of my interviews at this time and then give the parts pertaining to D-Day in the D-Day chapter.

Bradford Freeman Interview

I began my interview with Bradford C. Freeman by asking him to tell us about his enlistment.

BRADFORD FREEMAN: I enlisted on December.... I was sworn in on December 12, 1942. I didn't have to go to the service until April of 43.

JOHN LONG: Since you enlisted did you pick out the branch of service you wanted to go into?

BRADFORD FREEMAN: After I finished basic, I finished as infantry at Ft. McClellan Alabama. Whenever I finished there I volunteered for the paratroopers and then went to Benning and got my wings in November and went on up to Camp McCullough North Carolina.

We jumped a night jump that was the first ever night jump in training. I had jumped and then a plane over there fell out of the sky and killed about 19, so that is the reason why they gave me a 14 day leave to stop the jumping there for a time or two.

JOHN LONG: Do you have any recollection of what kind of pointed you towards being in the Airborne?

BRADFORD FREEMAN: Well the brother who finished just before I entered college, he joined the Airborne. He

55

was in the 11th Airborne. He jumped in the Pacific. We just decided we wanted to do it.

Well, the first thing we knew about it, the Germans had paratroopers before that and the Army and the Marines. The Army wanted paratroopers and the Marines wanted paratroopers so they had a jump in Florida, and the Army put out, I forget how many it was but it was two to their one, but anyway, so the Army got the paratroopers. That's the way it went, but I would have been in high school when they done that.

JOHN LONG: So the Marines wanted it but they didn't get it because the Army did a better job I guess.

BRADFORD FREEMAN: The way I understand it because they put more people on the ground in less time.

JOHN LONG: Is there anything that stands out in your mind about your early training when you first got in the Airborne; was there anything that you recall that would be worthwhile about mentioning in your early training in the Airborne?

BRADFORD FREEMAN: I was just glad to be there. I didn't think about the other.

JOHN LONG: Of course, being in the Airborne that is kind of like specialized training anyway, but outside of being in the Airborne did you have any other specialized training, such as in mortars?

BRADFORD FREEMAN: No, I got that in infantry. You got mortars, machine guns, BAR, M1, carbine, and a pistol. You got that in your infantry training, or I did.

JOHN LONG: About when did you find out they were going to ship you towards England?

BRADFORD FREEMAN: I trained with the 541st Parachute Regiment. They divided that up and shipped to

56

the 82nd to 101st and the 11th Airborne. They divided them up to bring them up to full strength. See, they didn't have full strength. That is what they told me was the reason. We trained up there in North Carolina, Camp McCullough, and we trained up there until, well I was entered foreign service on February 5th of 1944. Whenever I crossed over they unloaded us in Ireland.

JOHN LONG: Did you go over on a troop ship?

BRADFORD FREEMAN: No sir, it was on a grange ship. It was so small you had to get in your rack so your buddy could cross to get in his bed. We were stacked four high.

JOHN LONG: Did you get seasick like me on the way over.

BRADFORD FREEMAN: No sir, it didn't particularly bother me. Fact of being I hung up on a rail a lot. I always chewed tobacco so I would get out there and chew my tobacco and watch those little fish jumping. Did you see those little fish jump? There was always what they called those little flying fish right there beside you.

JOHN LONG: You say you landed in Ireland. At that time you weren't in the 506th then were you?

BRADFORD FREEMAN: No sir, I was just in the transport to wherever they wanted to send me and the 101st came and picked me up, not on a boat but a ferry I guess you call it.

JOHN LONG: When do you recall that you actually wound up in Easy Company with the 506th, Second Battalion?

BRADFORD FREEMAN: I don't remember exactly the date but it was, I say about a week after we landed in Ireland.

JOHN LONG: So shortly thereafter you wound up in Easy Company?

BRADFORD FREEMAN: Yes, sir.

JOHN LONG: What's your recollection about the type of training you received getting ready for D-Day? Was it about the same you had been receiving, kind of like repetition?

BRADFORD FREEMAN: That's all. It was just training. We trained for the same thing all the time. We had the training and they fired over us. We had fire. We crawled through things with the machine guns waving over you shooting over you. You know better than to put your head up under that wire, and all that kind of stuff.

JOHN LONG: That sounds like pretty standard. This might be a tough question. When did you realize that you were going to be part of something big and special like it turned out to be?

BRADFORD FREEMAN: Well we all knew that we were going to be in battle, because we were training for that purpose. I think every solider over there, I don't care what he was in, he knew that.

Joe Johnson Interview

I began my interview with Joe Johnson by asking him to tell us about himself.

JOE JOHNSON: My name is Joseph Ruben Johnson. I was born the 31st of May 1925. I was assigned to the 551st AAA Antiaircraft Automatic Weapons Battalion. I was a gunner on a 40mm bofor.

I was born in a little place called Goodway in Monroe County Alabama, south Alabama.

My father was a farmer. We had a big farm. There were 15 of us children, 8 boys and 7 girls. I begged my Daddy to sign with me so I could get into the military service, but my Daddy already had two boys in it and he said "Joseph I got enough boys in this war I don't want another one in it, so I said "Daddy, I need to go help them come home. "

JOHN LONG: Tell us about the time you was down in the field and you was worrying your Daddy and he said something about if you don't quit worrying me I am going to sign them papers.

JOE JOHNSON: I begged my Daddy to let me go in the service. I said "Daddy you need to sign and let me go in, and he said "Joseph, I'm not going to send you in that bloody war; that's a bloody war over there and I can't afford to do that."

One day I was aggravating him and he said "boy if you don't leave me alone I'm gonna sign them papers;" and man I really started on him then.

JOHN LONG: Where did you go for basic training?

JOE JOHNSON: The morning I left to go for my physical and be inducted in the military my Daddy said to me "Joe, you going to bloody war. Come in here." He was an elder in the Church of Jesus Christ of the Latter Day Saints. He had the priesthood and he gave me a priesthood blessing. He said, Joseph, if you listen to your commander and listen to the spirit and be a good soldier I promise you that you will return home, but you got to be a good soldier to do so.

JOHN LONG: Then you went to basic training?

JOE JOHNSON: I went for my physical to Anniston Alabama, Ft. McClenan Alabama. They fitted us up with all our uniforms and they had it on a big table and we were going down through there. You must remember I was on a farm, we didn't have many shoes. We went barefooted, and so I was going down the counter picking up my stuff and the guy had some shoes up there and I said what are these things, and he said you put them on your feet, and I said oh is that what happens. Is that where they go, I didn't know that. I was picking at him.

JOHN LONG: Okay, what kind of outfit did you train for?

JOE JOHNSON: I trained with the 551st AAA Antiaircraft Automatic Weapons.

JOHN LONG: After you completed your training in the United States you were shipped to England?

JOE JOHNSON: England, yeah.

JOHN LONG: About how long had you been in the military when you wound up in England?

JOE JOHNSON: Well, we took our basic training in a little place called Ft. Eustis Virginia, right out of Richmond VA, and as soon as we got done with the thirteen weeks of basic training they gave us a seven day leave and I went home.

When I got home there was a telegram there for me to report back because they had called my unit to deploy, so I went back. When I got there they were already gone to Camp Kilmer New Jersey.

I caught a train and went up to Camp Kilmer New Jersey and we processed the final process and got all our shots for overseas at Camp Kilmer and then we loaded on busses and went to Boston.

We shipped out of Boston MA on a British passenger liner. It was four schools and four stacks. That thing would do 32 knots. It would out run any submarine. It took us five days to go from Boston to Liverpool, where we dumped off on Liverpool.

JOHN LONG: That was fast because it normally takes two weeks.

JOE JOHNSON: Coming back it took us seventeen days on a cattle boat.

Eugene Meier Interview

I began my interview with Eugene Meier by asking him to tell us about himself.

EUGENE MEIER: I am 92 years old. I was on born January 6, 1921, in Hazelton Pennsylvania. When I graduated from high school in 1939 I had a desire to join the army. The mother was completely against it.

After I muddled around town for a while and helped my father in his business in 1941, in early 1942, I moved with some relatives in Philadelphia. I took a job with Westinghouse. I took an offer of the possibility of not being drafted. At that time I had not signed up for the draft yet because my birthday was in January 1921 and the next sign up was in the following June.

My cousin and I both worked in Westinghouse., and one day we were talking and we both decided that neither one of us were happy with what we were doing, with the war going on. We were talking about it and he said "hell, let's not talk about it, let's join." I said well what are you going to join and he said the Navy, so I said okay I will join the Navy with you.

We got ready one evening and went down to the Custom House in Philadelphia and enlisted in the Navy. We were both turned down because of a physical disorder, which was enough at that time to keep me out because of the Navy's strict standards. We both had an overbite in our teeth so we were both rejected.

We walked out into the hall, stood in front of the office, and I guess the recruiting officer told us to come back in two or three weeks, as they were going to change the standards. We stood out in the hall for two or three minutes and I said I don't think I want to wait so I go down the hall and join the Army.

I asked the fellow "when do I report" and he said tomorrow morning at 8:00 for a basic physical examination. Only bring with you the clothes that you are wearing and if you have any special toiletry items you are allowed to bring that in a small kit. Anyhow, I came back the next morning, I went through the physical and I came through with flying colors.

I said now what happens and he said hang around, there will be a bus here in an hour or two to take you to Ft. Meade in Maryland.

We got on the bus and went to Maryland. We were indoctrinated and issued our clothes and gave us all the normal rules, what to do, what not to do and all this kind of stuff and then we had to take a general aptitude battery test to see where we were going to go.

I had to laugh over that because to me all that did was if you had an extremely high occupation or talent you might have been put on a separate list, otherwise you were sent where the next batch of troops were going when your name came up.

Anyway, one by one we were loaded up on the train and sent to Ft. Belvoir Virginia to do our basic training. We finished our basic training.

On our first inspection, I was 21 at this time, our first inspection the officer came down the line and he grabbed my rifle out of my hands, he inspected it, pulled my rifle, he checked it to make sure there was no rust on it, so anyhow, everything was doing fine.

He handed my rifle back to me and he said "soldier, when did you shave last?" I said I am sorry sir but I have never shaved in my life. He said 'you are in the Army now" you will shave every morning whether you like it or not. I said yes sir, thank you and he moved on to the next recruit.

I said, well I passed that, I did well. I had the right answers. Anyhow, I completed the inspection and went all through the ceremonies and everything else that was involved in it and we were turned over to our officer in charge of the platoon. He in turn turned me over to the platoon Sergeant

He looked like a bulldog on the children's cartoons with steam coming out of his nostrils. I found out I did not have the right answers. Anyhow, he said you know everyone that passes inspection today has a three day pass over the weekend. I said yeah, I know, I am looking forward to it, and he said well don't, you are staying here.

Anyhow, we finished our basic training. We were issued 0.3 Springfield rifles, carry-overs from World War I. The helmets we wore were the old pipe clay type of helmet that they wore in World War I.

We had many air raid drills but there were nights we had to get up and go to the trenches on the outskirts of our building.

We finished our basic training. One morning, one by one they called out a list of names for us to be outside at a certain time with our duffle bags and then another list of names to be out maybe an hour later.

He went on down the list until all the names were gone and he said "okay dismissed." I went over to him and said "Sergeant, you didn't call my name" and he said you are not going anywhere so you stay here, so anyhow they sent me back into my barracks. We sat around for a day or two. Nothing was going on. There were about seven of us I

test battery and you have been selected to be candidates in the Officer Candidate School.

The first week in October, last of September we reported to a different building. We were assigned to Company Z. We began our travels and they turned us out as a 90 day wander. All I had under my waist, as military training was basic training and they are going to make an officer out of me.

I just couldn't understand this. It just didn't make sense so I mentioned it to the company commander at the school. I said hey here is my background, I don't feel as though I qualify and he said you are qualified or you wouldn't be here, now stop asking questions, so anyhow we went three months of extremely intensive training, extremely intensive.

We had a certain way to button our clothing that was hanging on the rack. If we went out and a tack officer came in and found a button open you gathered demerits.

We had all kinds of insults to us. They taught us that we were lower than worms and all this kind of stuff, and I think we had one that was just extreme in this case.

Anyhow, with all this intensive training, both in the field and in the classroom, physical exams it seemed like every other week, test exams every time we turned around and anyhow we finished our 90 days of training and we were commissioned Second Lieutenants in the Engineering Corp.

We were sent to Camp Claiborne Louisiana. While I was down there I was appointed as officer in charge, one of the officers in charge of the demolition range.

We were only there about six weeks and then again we loaded on a train and shipped over to Camp Swift in Texas. I was assigned inside as a desk officer, a staff officer, and that only lasted a few times then I was transferred to the 146th Engineer Regiment, 1st Battalion of the First Regiment.

In the week I was assigned to them we were separated out into two battalions.

We got our enlisted men from the draft board assignments. This was in February I think.

We were indoctrinated to the fact that we were combat engineers. We were the cream of the crop for the engineer corp. We got to England thinking, well here we are, we are combat engineers and we were assigned to the Assault Training Center.

The Assault Training Center was set up as Colonel Paul W. Thompson who was a 1909 graduate from West Point, or a little bit later maybe. While he was stationed in Berlin as military attaché for seven or eight years, he took a strong interest and made copious notes of both the French building a line and the Germans building a secret line.

He came back to this country and knowing what their capabilities were, the line of construction he was assigned in charge of the Assault Training Center. It was really set up with the 20th Engineers doing the labor work.

We took over for the 20th Engineers and our job was as each infantry regiment came through they were broken down on the platoon and then the company level and as they mastered each level of what they may be involved in on assault on foreign soil they moved on to the next, at the company level, the company moved the battalion.

They finally wound up after about five weeks doing on a regiment level, first the 29th. Several other divisions came through while we were there.

All we were just labor troops. We had nothing to do as engineers except for labor work. My platoon was assigned to an operating rock center, blowing rock loose and running the rocks through crushers and sent it out to the other units of our battalion because as these infantry troops are going through being taught these demolitions and these assaults on the pill boxes they would physically destroy the pill boxes that were set up for them to work on and they would move on.

The day they moved on to the next problem our men went in and they rebuilt the pill boxes, the barbed wire entanglement and everything else that was involved in it and this just recycled right on through until August, I forget the exact date. I'm sorry, not August but May, back at the end of July, end of April beginning of May they closed the Assault Training Center down because their units were finished.

We loaded up all of our equipment and moved to a town about fifty miles south to a little town right on the beach.

We unloaded on a Tuesday morning and on Wednesday afternoon we reloaded our truck and headed back up to the Assault Training Center and they told us that we had to take some special training. This is where we got our training in the use of demolition in the destroying of the beach obstacles that the Germans had strewed on the beach.

George Pulakos Interview

 I began my interview with George Pulakos by asking him to tell us how he felt about giving this interview.

JOHN LONG: Have you ever given an interview like this before?

GEORGE PULAKOS: No. Until maybe the last five or six years, nobody ever talked about the war and it wasn't until the news media when the fellow wrote the book about The Greatest Generation, and from then on people starting asking questions, but up until then I hadn't even told my sons. I told my sons just in the last year or two.

JOHN LONG: I think maybe you guys had thought that you didn't care to talk about it, but now maybe you realize maybe you should.

GEORGE PULAKOS: I think that's part of it; before nobody would approach you to even ask you about it.

JOHN LONG: If I understand it, you were more of a medic than anything else, right?

GEORGE PULAKOS: I enlisted and because I was in pre-med they put me in the enlisted reserve.

JOHN LONG: You already told me, earlier you said something about you being at Camp Pickett first?

GEORGE PULAKOS: Camp Pickett. At that time it was basic medical training. Of course, from there I went to Washington then from Washington to Georgetown and then all over.

JOHN LONG: Actually, did you wind up doing pretty well what you wanted to do?

GEORGE PULAKOS: More or less. I was interested in the medical field. At the time I was dead set on becoming a doctor, but I shouldn't tell you this, but dealing with surgeons I got disillusioned. Surgeons are a breed. They are the prima donnas.

When you have worked with surgeons; that discouraged me; I had no desire then to go back and finish school.

JOHN LONG: How did you, it sounds like you didn't adapt to military life too good?

GEORGE PULAKOS: I did alright. I enjoyed myself. I had a good time.

I started out, like I said I was in school for pre-med and I was actually draft exempt and my parents were rather happy about that. About the second year in school, I was young and foolish and thought I am going to miss something so I went and enlisted. I enlisted in the Army. They sent us down to opened up Camp Pickett, a brand new camp.

JOHN LONG: Where was that?

GEORGE PULAKOS: In Blackstone Virginia.

JOHN LONG: That name must have come from Pickett's Charge from Gettysburg.

GEORGE PULAKOS: I would imagine so, but we moved into it and our basic training in the beginning consisted of lining the ditches with pine logs.

Then I went out and they sent me to Walter Reed to go to surgical technician school, and I was just in there, half way through the course and they said that they looked at my background and schooling and said we are going to send you back to college, so they sent me to Georgetown University and they tested you to see what grade you were in, and I kept telling them, look I don't want to, that I had just enlisted out of college.

They said no, you have got to go through this so I said, I will fox them and I will just answer all the questions on the test and see where they are going to place me, I will just answer them all wrong. So when I got all through with the test, the guy looked at me and said nobody is this dumb. I am putting you in the first year of college at the University of Maryland.

JOHN LONG: That's a good story right there.

GEORGE PULAKOS: When I was out there I kept writing. Every week I wrote the commander and said I don't want to be here, I want to get out of here. They sent me from Washington DC to Georgetown right outside Washington to the University of Maryland, which is right outside of Washington and then they shipped me.

They finally said okay I will get you out of here and they sent me to Camp Grant Illinois as a replacement and they sent me back to Walter Reed and I went back into surgical technician and finished school and then they kept me there for a while to work surgery.

JOHN LONG: It sounds like you were dragged into being a medic kicking and squalling.

GEORGE PULAKOS: I was. I went through the Army as a PFC, but when you graduate surgical technician school you come out a Tech-Sergeant

The day that we finished school is when they had the graduation the next day. A buddy of mine and I thought we would climb the fence and go downtown Washington. At Walter Reed they have a rout iron fence about 8-feet high and then they have a hedge about 3-feet inside of that, a big high hedge.

It was winter time. We had these big Army overcoats and we threw them over the fence and went out and celebrated our finishing school and came back and threw our coats back over the fence and threw them over the bushes and then walked to the end of the bushes and two MPs were holding our coats.

They took us down, it was in the basement of the theater and there were a couple of cells down there and they put us in the cells and clanged the door shut.

I told the guy, I said you know if they forget about us someday somebody is going to come down here and find two skeletons.

Fortunately they came and got us out in the morning, but the fact they took us we were in deep trouble. They said we will graduate you, but you are going to graduate as a Private First Class. The rest of the class got Tech-Sergeant but we were PFC.

JOHN LONG: You got busted before you got the stripes then?

GEORGE PULAKOS: That was the beginning of my career with the Army. Then they sent us overseas, just a whole big group of medics and then we ended up in England.

JOHN LONG: How did you go over?

GEORGE PULAKOS: Went over on one of the liberty ships.

JOHN LONG: I got a famous question about that. Did you get seasick?

GEORGE PULAKOS: Nah. The closest I came to getting seasick was coming back. I came back on the Queen Mary.

It was very nice because I was with the hospital patients and had the main deck cabin.

Beautiful cabins, two to a cabin. No port hole, but it had like a window and I was lying in that bed.

The Queen Mary ran so fast that it didn't have escorts, but they shut off their gyro stabilizer because the submarines could hear it, so they ran without the stabilizer and I was lying in the bunk there one day and I said gee, we got a big roll here, and this is a big ship so I put my finger over there and I was following the horizon up and down, and all of a sudden I buried my head in the commode.

That's the closest I ever came to getting seasick, but that did it though.

JOHN LONG: When you got to England. Let's jump over a bit. You went over on a boat and got your training.

GEORGE PULAKOS: We landed in Liverpool and we progressively headed towards South Hampton. Of course, we had no idea what was going on at the time, but we ended up in a camp in South Hampton.

We thought we were in heaven. The mess halls were open 24 hours. You could go in and order anything you wanted. You could go to the PX and I think a carton of cigarettes cost us five cents.

We just thought this was great. We had no drills or nothing. Then, one evening they issued us, what they called invasion money.

JOHN LONG: They actually called it that?

GEORGE PULAKOS: Yeah, it was special money printed by the United States Government.

Earnest Wallace Interview

I began my interview with Earnest Wallace by asking him about himself and his enlistment.

EARNEST WALLACE: I was in the 101st Airborne, 2nd Battalion, 506th. I was squad leader in Fox Company.

JOHN LONG: Your full name?

EARNEST WALLACE: Earnest Bernard Wallace.

JOHN LONG: When were you born?

EARNEST WALLACE: January 13, 1920. I worked for a lumber company, a roofing job, in '38 until I enlisted in the Army. I was 22.

JOHN LONG: I believe you used the word enlisted, so you joined?

EARNEST WALLACE: Yeah, I enlisted in the Airborne. The reason I enlisted, before they drafted me. I was scared they would put me where I didn't want to go. I read in the paper that you would get $50 jump pay and that made my mind right up.

JOHN LONG: The extra $50?

EARNEST WALLACE: Yeah. I didn't care where I went; I just wanted to be in the paratroopers. Do you know that I stayed 72 days in Holland; 72 days, even without a bath? Holes would rot in our underwear they were so rotten.

When I got back they called us squad leaders in and said we were going up north, there was a bulge up there.

Me and the rest of the squad leaders, I had never heard of a bulge. I didn't know what it was. We got in those trucks and took off with great speed.

We went to Bastogne. I tell you a funny one there. When we got out at Bastogne, they told us to get on the side of the highway there and sit three men back to back; then we realized that something was coming up. Anyway, they called the sergeants down there.

The trucks were still there. They had white officers, and this young white officer was standing there and one of them colored men said, let's get out of here, and he said what's your hurry. He said sir, wherever these paratroopers go all hell is going to break loose.

JOHN LONG: Tell me more about Holland.

EARNEST WALLACE: Up in Holland. We run up and down them highways and on that dike for 72 days and we did not get a bath. They deloused us, burned our clothes, and brought portable showers in and put it in the Rhine River there.

Them first boys, troopers that took a bath, they used all the hot water. When I got home I would take two baths a day.

My mama thought I was crazy. When me and Jerrie got married the skin still wasn't right on my legs. I got hit in Normandy with shrapnel and it got infected there. I had to go all them years, months, and I got pieces of metal out of me after I got married.

JOHN LONG: That doesn't sound too good. We'll talk more about that later. Let's go back to Holland.

EARNEST WALLACE: I got wounded in Holland at the windmill. It hit me in the face and chipped my front tooth. That's the only time I went on sick call. It hit me in the face. I was so numb and it frightened me very, very much. I had a good buddy that had dug a hole there.

The dike was as big as this house, much bigger with a highway on top of it. I got to…. and I said "am I hit bad?"

See, all I could see was blood, and he said awe you alright and he talked to me and I got alright then, but I could have died with fright I guess.

JOHN LONG: Well, let's back up a little bit now. I am going down this list here, and before we get into Normandy and jumping in and going on to Bastogne and Holland, we want to talk about your training and where you trained, and any kind of special training.

EARNEST WALLACE: Well, we went to Ft. Walton Texas, right out of Houston. Then we left Camp Walton to go to Ft. Benning, and the first thing that they done is you didn't walk you double timed everywhere but the mess hall.

The first meal the mess sergeant came out to where we were eating and wanted to know if anybody was from Charlotte. Of course me and another one said we were and he came over and talked to us. I knew some people he knew, but anyway when he got ready to leave, he said don't let Oscar frighten you.

I thought Oscar was a Sergeant; anyway the next morning we went up there to a field. It was way down, a valley like and we was up there and they had benches up there and all them men that flew this class sat down. Four planes took off and came over and made a jump. There were two streamers. Do you know what a streamer is?

JOHN LONG: Not exactly.

EARNEST WALLACE: Chutes not open. The ambulance came out there, picked them up and took them back. That officer that was doing the talking said that don't happen but just every now and then, and he said now if you don't want to get in this outfit you gonna have to get up and walk back. Well several of them got up and walked back.

JOHN LONG: I imagine so. Well, what was Oscar?

EARNEST WALLACE: Oscar was a dummy. They had wired the chute and they took us down in the hangers and Oscar was a dummy.

JOHN LONG: Is that what the two streamers were?

EARNEST WALLACE: Yeah. They was in the streamers, out of the chutes. You double timed five miles out every morning and five miles back after breakfast. I don't remember, but I believe we had a bath and then went to breakfast and then all day long, and in that place, you know it got hot down there. That double timing, we had to double time everywhere.

JOHN LONG: Did they have you double timing and clapping your hands too?

EARNEST WALLACE: Yeah.

JOHN LONG: They still done it to me too. Let me ask you this now. This is kind of like something I want to be clear about, because it's good. It sounds like the mess sergeant that you talked to said don't let Oscar frighten you, was talking about these streamers with the dummies.

EARNEST WALLACE: Yeah, that's what he was talking about. I didn't know that until they told us down there when we went in the hangers and seen the dummies and the wired up chutes where it wouldn't open and they said "this is Oscar." That's when we found out what he was talking about.

JOHN LONG: When the streamers come down it looked like real fellows coming down...

EARNEST WALLACE: That's exactly right, and the ambulance came out and picked them up and took off back somewhere.

JOHN LONG: So it sounds like they had it set up to see who had it to stay and who all really didn't want to stay. It was kind of like a set up deal.

EARNEST WALLACE: It was a set up deal. The next thing they done to us, they had a platform way up there and it had a cable going down to a bunch of sawdust and we put a harness on and they showed us how to go out the door, turn our butt towards the prop of the frame, you know the propeller, to where it opened, hit the chute and open it up.

JOHN LONG: That back wind would hit you.

EARNEST WALLACE: Yeah. When you go out the door you go out to your right, well that front blast helped open the chute I guess that's the reason. A lot of the boys got up there and were frightened. It was funny.

JOHN LONG: They didn't want to jump?

EARNEST WALLACE: They refused.

JOHN LONG: Was this out of the plane?

EARNEST WALLACE: No, this was off that platform. We hadn't made a jump then.

JOHN LONG: Let me tell you what Mr. Freeman told me. He said he liked to chew tobacco and they told him not to chew no tobacco when he was jumping off that tower, well, he jumped with a big chew and he got hung upside down and he said he don't know to this day whether he swallowed that chewing tobacco or spit it out.

EARNEST WALLACE: Let me tell you about my experience with it. They wouldn't let us have any water on them five mile double times out and five back. One of them boys chewed Beech Nut tobacco in my company. I can't remember his name. He told me, now I am going to roll this up and you put it in your mouth but don't chew it and you won't get thirsty.

Well, I believed him. Well, on that little road, it went down, there was a little creek thing that had water in it going down that little road, and every now and then I would hit it a lick. After a while I got to chewing it, I got deathly sick and I took off right down to that creek and I stuck my head in the creek. That made me sick.

JOHN LONG: You didn't chew any more tobacco did you?

EARNEST WALLACE: No, not until about ten years ago.

JOHN LONG: It took him a while to get over that first chew. Can you think of anymore about the training they put on you?

EARNEST WALLACE: No, but the training in the evening was really tough, very tough.

JOHN LONG: Before we get to England, did they give you any what they call specialized training to maybe handle mortars, or....

EARNEST WALLACE: Oh yeah, You learned that in basic training. I went in so early I was trained with a 0.3 rifle, a World War I rifle. We marched with sticks. They had a few machine guns and we trained with machine guns, World War II machine guns that was different in World War II.

JOHN LONG: Let me ask you this one. How many jumps...I am not talking about the tower, how many actual jumps did you make before you had to do the real thing?

EARNEST WALLACE: I got credit for 22 jumps and 2 combat jumps.

Harold Powers Interview

You were drafted in September of 1942 and asked to be a paratrooper. Tell us about that.

HAROLD POWERS: They sent us up to Fort Knox and we had basic training there in the tank company and what have you and I went to supply school while I was there; and then they shipped us to Camp Campbell Kentucky but now it's called Fort Campbell.

JOHN LONG: After you left Ft. Campbell where did you go?

HAROLD POWERS: I volunteered for the paratroopers and was sent to Ft. Benning Georgia for jump training there.

JOHN LONG: After you got your Airborne training at Ft. Benning then what happened to you?

HAROLD POWERS: We went on maneuvers and then we shipped out from Boston to England.

JOHN LONG: Did you go over on a troop ship?

HAROLD POWERS: Yeah.

JOHN LONG: Paratrooper on a troop ship. I would have thought they would have flown you over there.

HAROLD POWERS: I would have thought they would have too. It would have been nice if they did, but you wasn't sure those planes could go that far.

JOHN LONG: Did you get seasick?

HAROLD POWERS: It didn't bother me at all.

JOHN LONG: Tell us a little about getting used to being in the Airborne, your barracks life and that sort of thing before we go into detail.

HAROLD POWERS: Well, when you went to Ft. Benning you had to pack your own chutes there, and of course you went through the rigorous training they had, physical training and what have you, and you had to make five jumps and you pack the chutes. Of course you had a partner and you packed his and of course he helped me pack mine.

JOHN LONG: In Normandy you each had two chutes. Did you each work together on both of them?

HAROLD POWERS: No. We didn't have to pack the reserve chute. It was just a small one that fit in front of you.

JOHN LONG: Was that jumping off towers?

HAROLD POWERS: Off of towers and getting used to the jerk.

JOHN LONG: Where did you make your first actual jump out of an airplane?

HAROLD POWERS: Down at Ft. Benning.

JOHN LONG: In your training, how many jumps out of an airplane did you have to make?

HAROLD POWERS: I think I ended up with around 12.

JOHN LONG: This other fellow, in the 506th, they called themselves the Band of Brothers. In the 501st you said you called yourselves Geronimo?

HAROLD POWERS: Yeah, we hollered Geronimo and all that when you jumped out of a plane, but we had one fellow that the story about Saving Private Ryan was in my Regiment or Battalion really.

JOHN LONG: Tell us a little bit about your recollections about being in England before you left out for the invasion process.

HAROLD POWERS: Well it was just more training you know, until we got ready to go. It was a few days before we took off on D-Day. We studied maps and sandboxes of the areas that we were supposed to land in.

JOHN LONG: Did you have any specific recollections of what you guys did when you were not training in England?

HAROLD POWERS: I took a flight on a glider, went to London, went to Oxford and places like that when you got a pass to go.

JOHN LONG: One fellow when I asked that question he said that most of the guys set around and played poker and shot craps.

HAROLD POWERS: Nah, I didn't do that.

* * *

So eight of our 14 Hero Interviewees were now in the war.

Churchill and Stalin had a new partner and we had a real World War.

The Big Three Churchill, Roosevelt and Stalin began to plan the war together:

One of their first joint decisions was to concentrate on Hitler in Europe and leave the Pacific for later. The rationalization was based on the strength and potential danger from Hitler.

Roosevelt knew that he could get disagreement from home since Japan had attacked the US; but he recognized and agreed that they had to go after Hitler first.

Later in their discussions Stalin started urging them to think about plans after the war. He wanted them to begin planning for how Europe would be divided after the war ended.

This was the prelude to the Cold War that would follow World War II.

***

The first US soldiers arrived in England in January 1942.

The Army Air Force personnel arrived in April and May.

The B-24 Liberator was one of the first US planes to arrive in Great Britain.

Hitler shifted his primary goal from an immediate victory in Russia to the more long-term goal of securing the southern Soviet Union's oil fields for his was machine. But he remained on the offensive.

Germany intensified their Blitz against England.

German Field Marshal Erwin Rommel's Afrika Korps in North Africa captured Tobruk in June.

But now the Allies began to bomb Germany. They hit
Cologne with the first ever thousand-bomber air raid.

Germany retaliates by bombing British cathedral cities.

Germany's Japanese allies continued their expansion into
Borneo, Java and Sumatra. The British fortress of
Singapore fell rapidly in February.

The Japanese took about 25,000 prisoners, many of which
would later die in Japanese camps.

This was the year of the peak of Japanese expansion. But
the Battle of Midway turned that around. US sea-based
aircraft destroyed four Japanese carriers and a cruiser.

Chapter 3
Hitler Starts Losing

Germany's fortunes were also turned around in the second half of the year. British forces led by Montgomery defeated German forces and gained the initiative in North Africa at El Alamein.

Russian forces counterattacked at Stalingrad.

The Russian counter attack at Stalingrad was effective. Germany surrendered at Stalingrad February 2, 1942 and this began to turn the war around.

It was the first major defeat of Hitler's armies.

It had cost the Russians 2.5 million casualties.

War continued to rage in the Atlantic. German U boats sank 27 merchant vessels in a 4 day period.

But by the end of May, the Battle of the Atlantic was effectively over.

Enigma Code Breaking

The British code breakers at Bletchley and the effectiveness of long range bombers inflicted enormous losses on the U-boats.

Enough can not be said about the effectiveness of the code breakers. Some have estimated that their code breaking shortened the war by 2 to 4 years.

The German coding machine named Enigma is an interesting story unto itself.

The German engineer Arthur Scherbius developed the Enigma machine with the hope of using it commercially for coding and decoding secure communications. He began to manufacture it in 1923 in his Cipher Machines Corporation in Berlin.

Within three years the German navy was producing its own version, followed by the army in 1928 and the air force in 1933.

Enigmas allowed an operator to type in a message, and then scramble it by using three to five notched wheels, or rotors, which displayed different letters of the alphabet.

The receiver needed to know the exact settings of these rotors in order to reconstitute the coded text. Over the years the basic machine became more complicated as German code experts added plugs with electronic circuits.

Britain and her allies first began to understand the Enigma machine in 1931 when a German spy allowed his French spymasters to photograph stolen Enigma operating manuals.

It was only after they had handed over details to the Polish Cipher Bureau that progress was made. Helped by its closer links to the German engineering industry, the Poles managed to reconstruct an Enigma machine, complete with internal wiring, to read the German forces' messages between 1933 and 1938.

With German invasion imminent in 1939, the Poles opted to share their secrets with the British.

The Germans were convinced that Enigma output could not be broken, so they used the machine for all sorts of communications on the battlefield, at sea, in the sky and, significantly, within its secret services.

Britain only allowed a select few commanders to be aware that Britain had developed the ability to decode the German messages. They used Enigma sparingly to prevent the Germans from realizing that their ciphers had been broken.

Enigma Code Breaker

Germany Retreats

German Admiral Donitz withdrew the German fleet from the contended areas

In mid-May German and Italian forces in North Africa surrendered to the Allies.

By the end of May Mussolini had fallen.

In September the Italians surrendered to the Allies.

This surrender prompted the Germans to invade northern Italy and a German task force rescued Mussolini and established a fascist republic in North Italy.

As the Russian advance on the Eastern Front gathered pace, recapturing Kharkov and Kiev from Germany, Allied bombers began to attack German cities in enormous daylight air raids.

The opening of the Second Front in Europe, long discussed and always postponed, was being prepared for the following year.

The Soviets, in 1943 were able to reclaim half of the territory taken by the Germans in 1941 and 1942.

The Big Three: Stalin, Roosevelt and Churchill met at Tehran in November 1943 to continue their planning.

The parties later agreed that Britain and America would launch a cross-channel invasion of France in May 1944 and a separate invasion of southern France.

The Soviet Union continued to make significant advances across Eastern Europe toward Germany.

The draft enabled the US Army to grow to 5,400,888 by the end of 1943. Five of our Interviewees were included in this draft.

Jack Carver Interview

I began the interview with Jack Carver by asking him to tell us how he wound up in the military. Did you join or get drafted?

JACK CARVER: Well, I was thinking about joining but I got my thing to report to Hattiesburg.

JOHN LONG: To Camp Shelby?

JACK CARVER: Camp Shelby. I got down there and I told them I wanted the Air Force, but they said they can't guarantee nothing, but anyway, after a few days, I wasn't there very long, they put us on a train and that train left Hattiesburg and wound up in New Jersey, but they didn't go straight.

They went down around through Florida and up the coast around there. I wound up in Atlantic City, New Jersey. We lived in a hotel there right on the Boardwalk; had this about a 10 to 12 foot story hotel. We lived on the eighth floor I think. That's where we did our training.

We would come down and we go out somewhere and march a little bit. When it was too bad up there they had this big building; they said it was big enough to play some kind of a ballgame in and we would go there sometime when the weather was real bad.

This was in the winter time when it was real cold and everything. That's where I went to take my basic at.

JOHN LONG: Does that article say what date he actually went in?

JACK CARVER: No. It just says "I entered in 1943."

JOHN LONG: You got your summons and was drafted in 1943, do you remember what date it was in '43 that you first had to report and be sworn in?

JACK CARVER: No I really don't. I don't remember.

JOHN LONG: That's alright. Even though you were drafted you asked for the Air Force, but wound up…

JACK CARVER: Actually, when I left Atlantic City they sent me to this school in Flint Michigan for 1830, Pratt was putting engines on the airplanes so I said well I don't get the Air Force.

Well, I got up there, and had never even been close to an airplane before you know, but we didn't have any airplanes, we just worked with Buick Motors in Flint, Michigan, that's where I went to school at. I went through and made it through school and they turned me loose. We didn't have an airplane to check on.

JOHN LONG: This question, kind of like goes around. What kind of training did you have to begin with and did you get some specialized training later on and so forth?

JACK CARVER: Well, yeah. When I did get to go they sent me to Ft. Benning Georgia the next time. Ft. Benning, they had paratroopers down there too at Ft. Benning. They carried me down there.

It was down a hill, down there where the river was. It had a flat spot and an Air Base, and they had a C-47 airplane.

They pulled it up there and they said "now this is yours to take care of". I have never been in one before in my life. I knew about the engines but that's it. I said, well where do you put gas in it, about the wings? They thought I was crazy.

JOHN LONG: It's kind of funny how they just give you something to see after and you ain't got no...

JACK CARVER: Yeah, told me you take care of it.

JOHN LONG: So you got some kind of specialized training at Ft. Benning?

JACK CARVER: Well, not really specialized. We got there and then we moved from there to Grenada, Mississippi, and I was so glad of it. That was right before I had to go overseas.

When I got moved there I could go home. It ain't but about 10 miles from Grenada down to where I lived in the county there, and I got to go home a few times while I was in Grenada. We did do a lot of training there, just flying around, training the crews on the airplane.

JOHN LONG: Sounds like your guardian angel was looking after you. You asked for the Air Force and you got that, and then you wound up pretty close to your house.

JACK CARVER: From there, they said, well you are going to get you an airplane. They got me and a pilot.

There was me, a pilot and a co-pilot. They sent us up to Ft. Wayne, Indiana. We went up and got an airplane. See, they was burying planes over there; all kinds of airplanes.

Anybody that went over there would see an airplane. So me and the pilot and the co-pilot we carried this C-47. We

95

went to West Palm Beach and down across the Salem route they called it, down to Puerto Rico and across there.

They had a little ole bitty island out there, somewhere out there. I never had heard about it. They say it is about as big as, maybe three or four acres. Which that's all there was out in the middle of the ocean there.

You got to stop out there and get some gas too when you are going through there, and they put a navigator on that airplane with us. He kept up with right where we were, and I was glad to see him.

We had four big tanks put in that airplane, full of gas to carry over there. I was afraid we were going to miss that little island out there. If we had we wouldn't have had enough gas to get to the next place, but we did and we made it.

JOHN LONG: I see now why you were so glad to put a navigator on there.

JACK CARVER: It was a little spot out there in the ocean.

JOHN LONG: Here is kind of like a generalized thing that they ask; about you're adapting to military life and the barracks and the food, and how you went from being a civilian into how the way the military does.

JACK CARVER: That's when I really got into the military part of it, when I got to England. I was assigned to that and then I was assigned an airplane to take care of and fly in, so that's where I got my specialized training, being in the service really, because the other places was just a school and different things.

JOHN LONG: Especially starting off in an Atlantic City Hotel. That doesn't sound like the military to me. [Laughs] So, you really didn't soldier until you got to England?

JACK CARVER: That's about how it looks.

JOHN LONG: That's where you got the special training for the gliders?

JACK CARVER: Well nah, I didn't get no special training for it; they just put us onto a glider and we carried it over there. That's all we did. I didn't do nothing with the gliders. We just carried them over there to Germany and dropped them off.

JOHN LONG: Do you remember what part of England you were in for the biggest part, in England? Where was you? Like what area, what town was close by or anything?

JACK CARVER: I know, but I don't...Merrifield seems like that's a name they had, something about Merrifield. I remember when we all got airplanes there were C47s lined up from here to yonder, and the troops...when they were going in for the invasion of Normandy, we were right on the coast there.

JOHN LONG: Most of the guys talked about Plymouth England.

JACK CARVER: Seems like that's about where it was because there was a bunch of people and a bunch of airplanes. I didn't know they had that many airplanes.

Olin Baxter McKee Interview

 Olin Baxter McKee was born June 20, 1923 and was drafted at age 19. He was assigned to the 266th Field Artillery Battalion; he was the youngest man in his company. He rose to the rank of First Sergeant

OLIN BAXTER MCKEE was involved in five campaigns, beginning with Normandy, Northern France, The Ardennes, Rhineland, and ultimately Central Europe. He was in charge of a Howitzer that fired a 360 lb. pound projectile for a range of 14 miles. That was the biggest gun that our country had at that particular time.

JOHN LONG: Was that particular artillery piece bigger and shoot further than anything the other side had?

OLIN MCKEE: As far as I know.

JOHN LONG: Were you drafted?

OLIN MCKEE: Yes, sir. My brother and I went in a day apart, I think…we left the 19th and 20th of January, but according to my military records I was inducted January 23, 1943.

JOHN LONG: That's what we got to go by, your DD214. When you got drafted kind of give us a chronological order of where they sent you and what you did.

OLIN MCKEE: Ft. Bragg, then I was shipped to New York. That is where I boarded the Queen Mary.

JOHN LONG: So you actually trained mostly in Ft. Bragg? The artillery area is usually Ft. Sill, Oklahoma. A lot of the artillery was in Ft. Sill.

OLIN MCKEE: I think I forgot more than I remember.

JOHN LONG: That's okay.

OLIN MCKEE: We had some training at Ft. Bragg before we shipped out.

JOHN LONG: I know your basic training don't deal with what your MOS winds up being. Did you do any artillery training per say before you went over to England or did you do your artillery training after you got there?

OLIN MCKEE: We did some training there on mortars and other guns. They had me capable of filling in just about anything pertaining to the guns.

JOHN LONG: We will bring that up when we get down into that area. I understand you were there 20 days past D-Day and then right on through The Ardennes, all the way to the end of the war.

JOHN LONG: When you went over on the Queen Mary, did you get seasick?

OLIN MCKEE: I don't think I got real sick, but queasy.

JOHN LONG: Generally speaking, how would you say you adapted from being a civilian and working in business and now you are in the Army and you got to snap too and all that?

OLIN MCKEE: I have always, before and after and even up to now done the best I could with what I had to do with. I was just in the business here, in the building business, and I don't mean to brag or anything but it done very well. I have always been able to adapt to whatever I had to do. I did the best I could with what I had.

JOHN LONG: Describe, if you will, the time that you spent in England before you got on the barge or whatever it was that brought you to Omaha Beach.

OLIN MCKEE: Well, I don't remember too much about it, except that my outfit was very good to try to agree and adapt to wherever we were. They were very friendly. As most people would, most men, we tried to meet as many people as we could.

JOHN LONG: You said a while ago that your commanding officers were pretty good group.

OLIN MCKEE: They were good officers. Yes, sir. Very good officers.

JOHN LONG: Tell us something about them.

A. Well, if I can remember their names. One of their names was Chuck Guise, I think is the way he spelled it.

JOHN LONG: Was he a Captain?

OLIN MCKEE: Lieutenant at that time. Captain Fernando was...

JOHN LONG: That's alright about names. I can't remember people's names I have known all my life sometimes. But anyway, overall your COs were highly attuned to your problems and so forth?

OLIN MCKEE: Yes, sir; Very good officers.

JOHN LONG: Do you recall any specific times that you spent with the people in England while you were training and maybe off duty? For example, I had one fellow that talked about all they did was shoot craps and play poker on their off time and then one fellow said he didn't do that, that he went in town and met some English folks and they would take him in for supper and all that kind of stuff.

OLIN MCKEE: No, sir, I didn't have that experience.

JOHN LONG: Did they keep you pinned up before D-Day; like they did somebody put you in a wired group where you couldn't go out?

OLIN MCKEE: We were restricted for about a week before we went out, if I remember correctly.

JOHN LONG: Did you ever come to the realization that you were in the middle of something big?

OLIN MCKEE: Stayed like that.

JOHN LONG: Did you ever get the feeling that this is going to be an event that is going to be historical as much as it was?

OLIN MCKEE: Well of course we knew that and we just adapted to it and accepted it. All in all we had a real good bunch of men. We had one fellow that went AWOL. He lived above Charlotte and he liked to drink a good bit and he took one too many and went home.

For some reason, I don't even remember until today, when something like that came up the captain would call me for some reason because I knew that whole area and lived in Charlotte my whole life. They would send me out to get him. I would have to go get him out of jail and bring him back and sober him up.

JOHN LONG: Let's come down to the actual time, and based on what I have learned so far is, that D-Day was actually supposed to be the day before and the weather was so bad that Eisenhower put it off a day. Do you recall that aspect of it?

OLIN MCKEE: Yes. I remember all of that.

JOHN LONG: Give me your best description....

OLIN MCKEE: The guns, of course we called it the tube and the barrel. You separated it and there was a piece you put on when you arrived at the destination to prepare to fire.

JOHN LONG: Was this particular artillery piece self-propelled or was it drawn? Was it pulled by a truck or tank or something?

OLIN MCKEE: It was pulled. It had wheels on it and we could pull it.

JOHN LONG: Kind of like a trailer?

OLIN MCKEE: Right. They were good guns. We had good results from them. It took, if I remember right, two men to load them, 300 and something pound shells and it had like a tray and you get the bullets so to speak and carry them to the gun and shove them in.

JOHN LONG: If I get the picture right then, the shell was placed in a tray and that tray would slide right up into the chamber.

OLIN MCKEE: Right, of course we would have to push it in.

Percy Scarborough Interview

Percy Scarborough was drafted in September of 1943. He received basic training at Camp Shelby, Fort Campbell Kentucky and Blanding Florida for the infantry.

He was shipped to England on the French Merchant Marines, the E.B. Alexander.

I asked him when he first realized he was training for the invasion.

PERCY SCARBOROUGH: It was actually when we went to England we knew we were part of the overall thing, but didn't know the extent or anything of it.

JOHN LONG: Is there anything that you would like to tell us about your experiences before you left out from England? There was lots of things going on. One bunch said they put them in jail, in effect, a stockade they had

102

with Constantia wire around it and couldn't nobody go out nowhere.

PERCY SCARBOROUGH: Oh no, we were on the highest hill in England. It was up above what we called a tent city. It was probably 15,000 or 20,000 troops there on top of this hill.

JOHN LONG: At this time, what was the outfit you were in?

PERCY SCARBOROUGH: I was not attached to anything at that particular time.

JOHN LONG: In England?

PERCY SCARBOROUGH: I was attached to the 90th Infantry about a week before we went in.

JOHN LONG: Was you training on the mortar before you went in?

PERCY SCARBOROUGH: Yeah.

JOHN LONG: So you were already trained in that aspect? With regard to the mortar itself, you got an elevation and you got right and left, and everything else, how did ya'll figure that on that particular type mortar?

PERCY SCARBOROUGH: We would fire one round then the forward observation with the binoculars would tell him where he wanted to go, 20 degrees right or 10 degrees left, back or forward. Back would give you more height and forward would shorten it down. But it was the man with the binoculars that you set your gun sights for him and he would say 20 degrees right...

JOHN LONG: He was the FO.

PERCY SCARBOROUGH: Forward observer.

JOHN LONG: See, I was in a mortar outfit.

PERCY SCARBOROUGH: In which I switched from gunner to forward observer off and on.

JOHN LONG: Well out of the two places I believe I would rather be up on the gun than up on, observing, you know. Wrong?

PERCY SCARBOROUGH: No, you got to savage more when you were on front.

JOHN LONG: And, if you weren't around the mortars you would be less apt to get something dropped on you as if you were up there being an observer. Is that right?

PERCY SCARBOROUGH: Right.

JOHN LONG: The first thing that pops in my mind is, you don't want to be on the front line you would rather be back, but there is more danger in the back part with a mortar because they want to take them out.

PERCY SCARBOROUGH: And they did their best to take them out.

JOHN LONG: Did you have any fun when you were in England?

PERCY SCARBOROUGH: Oh yeah. I enjoyed the different types of dances that they put on.

JOHN LONG: Do you have any particular fond memories of what you experienced before the invasion, you know like maybe you ran into somebody?

PERCY SCARBOROUGH: Not really. They had a pretty tight rein on us when we were in England.

JOHN LONG: Wasn't too much partying going on?

PERCY SCARBOROUGH: No, we did some pretty serious training.

JOHN LONG: There wasn't much fun and games when you was training, that's for sure.

PERCY SCARBOROUGH: I eat a lot of green eggs. I had never eat a green egg. Of course they fed us before daylight and unless you had a match or something you didn't know what you were eating.

Ivy Agee Interview

Ivy Agee was drafted and sent to Camp Forest then to Fort Sill, Oklahoma for training.

I asked if that was for artillery training.

IVY AGEE: The artillery school. That's where I took all my basics. After my basic raining I was on my way to England. I didn't even get a furlough home, a pass or anything. They said Mr. Agee you don't need a pass; you need to get in this war.

JOHN LONG: Did you have any family members in the service?

IVY AGEE: I didn't have any brothers or sisters. I was the only child.

JOHN LONG: What did your folks think about you getting drafted and sent to England?

IVY AGEE: Well, you know how they are, they was all crying and everything when I left.

JOHN LONG: According to this you went from Fort Sill Oklahoma to Plymouth England.

IVY AGEE: It was six weeks of basic training; and then some more when I got to England.

JOHN LONG: What ship did you go over on?

IVY AGEE: I went on Queen Elizabeth. It took four days to go and came back on the John W. Brown; it took 17 days to come back.

JOHN LONG: They got you over there quick but they wasn't in no rush to get you back.

IVY AGEE: They was in no hurry to get me home.

JOHN LONG: What happened next?

IVY AGEE: We had an air raid, first one of them. We didn't know where to go even. We got outside and the sky was just as light as day nearly; they dropped flares. They said follow the old guys so that's what we did.

IVY AGEE: We went out in what they call Moors over there. They had a lot of swamps in them Moors. If you got the jeep or one of those vehicles in one of them swampy places it was hard to get out. You tried it and you just keep going deeper and deeper.

JOHN LONG: I don't know whether it's a good question or not, but when you wasn't training, what were you doing, like in your idle time?

IVY AGEE: I would go downtown sometime. I was down there one night and they had an air raid. I went outside and it was just as light outside. They dropped flares you know. Going back up to camp I had to go up a hill all the way. A lot of times I would catch one of those little buses, two-deckers you know and would go up the hill in it.

JOHN LONG: About how long did you train before D-Day? In other words, about how long, was it like two or three months?

IVY AGEE: It was about six months I guess; nah, probably over a year. I forget those things.

JOHN LONG: You think you were in England over a year?

IVY AGEE: Yeah, I went to England and stayed in England until D-Day. We would go to Plymouth and sit on a rock wall down there and look across at France and think how far I was away from home and how soon it would be before I would be landing on those banks.

JOHN LONG: So you could go down there, like the Cliffs of Dover or somewhere like that and see across.

IVY AGEE: Yeah, sit down there and think about home and things.

James Springer Interview

James Springer was drafted and served in the infantry where he rose to Staff Sergeant. When I interviewed him he was 93 years old and frail. I began with some personal questions.

JOHN LONG: If I understand it right, you were married before you had to go into the service, is that correct?

JAMES SPRINGER: Yeah, but my daughter wasn't born until I was in Germany. I can talk hardly.

JOHN LONG: Yes sir, I see that. If you get to the point where it becomes a strain on you, you let me know and we will call a halt to it. Alright sir: how old are you now?

JAMES SPRINGER: 93.

JOHN LONG: Where did you report to when you were drafted?

JAMES SPRINGER: Ft. Benning, Georgia.

JOHN LONG: When did you know that you were going to have to go to England and go overseas and so forth?

JAMES SPRINGER: We got our training and then I went to Camp McCoy, Wisconsin and there is where I trained. From there we went when we got orders, overseas and did a 25 mile hike and we got on a troop ship and joined the convoy over to England... Ireland. We started our training and went to Whales and trained.

JOHN LONG: What particular training did they give you?

JAMES SPRINGER: I was just a rifleman in a squad.

***

I will pick up the interviews with our Hero Interviewees and their D-Day activities after I provide a general overview of D-Day.

Chapter 4
D-Day

"You are about to embark upon the Great Crusade, toward which we have striven these many months. The eyes of the world are upon you. The hopes and prayers of liberty-loving people everywhere march with you."
General Dwight D. Eisenhower, June 6, 1944

Japan began its last offensive in China in 1944 and captured additional territory in the south to add to its previous acquisitions.

Their control was limited however, to the major cities and lines of communication due to the effectiveness of the resistance of the Chinese Communists.

Germans finally retreated from Anzio at the end of May due to the Allied advance in Italy.

Rome was liberated in June, the day before the Allies' D-Day landings.

On 6 June, D-Day, over 130,000 Allied forces landed on five Normandy beaches: codenamed Utah, Omaha, Gold, Juno and Sword.

Some 12,000 aircraft ensured air superiority for the Allies. They bombed German defenses and provided cover for the troops.

The beaches of Normandy were chosen for the invasion because they lay within range of air cover and were less heavily defended than the obvious objective of the Pas de Calais, for which the Germans had set up the strongest defenses.

Six divisions landed on D-Day; three U.S., two British and one Canadian.

Two additional British and one U.S. division followed after the assault divisions had cleared the beach defenses.

But the airborne troops were the first to see action on D-Day. Their mission was to disrupt and confuse the Germans so as to prevent a concentrated counterattack against the seaborne troops coming in at dawn, and to protect the flanks of the invasion force at Sword and Utah beaches.

Three airborne divisions, two American and one British, dropped behind the landing beaches in the hours before dawn.

Over 20,000 men, the largest airborne force ever assembled, entered Normandy by glider and parachute.

The British 6th Airborne Division dropped to the east of the landing beaches to secure the flank and destroy several bridges to prevent the Germans from bringing up reinforcements.

The US 82nd and 101st Airborne Divisions dropped to the west.

Five of our Hero Interviewees participated in this air drop.

William Fasking Interview Continued

William Fasking was assigned as a glider pilot in the early morning invasion on D-Day.

I asked him to recount his memories of that day when he flew an English glider rather than the type of glider for which he had initially been trained.

WILLIAM FASKING: Well yeah. That was the Horsa glider that I flew into Normandy. That was an English glider. I got a lot of time to test that.

I landed with the brakes locked and figured on the skid marks there on the dirt I figured how long I would go landing at the lowest speed I could and about 600 feet so I had a pretty good idea of the fields that we went into if I could land them with the brakes locked and stop in time or if I would have to find some other tactic in slowing down.

I did, eventually, when we landed over there in Normandy, the Airborne Lieutenant, I was in a Horsa glider and had a trailer load of ammunition and 13 troops.

Anyway this lieutenant was looking over my shoulder and the field I was supposed to go into and the one I had planned on; was only one glider in it, and didn't seem like anything.

There was one guy laying on the ground out there but there didn't seem to be anything else there, and I just started to turn in there and he said, "any place but there" so I just flipped her around to the right.

There was another little field there about 500 feet so I figured I could get it in there and knock the gear off.

After he told me that instead of going and sitting down.... To begin with, he told all the troops whatever you do sit in your seats.

I told them. I told him. I told everybody. I kept repeating that stuff all the time. You are better off sitting in the seat and I will be damn he was still standing there and I kicked that thing sideways and tried to knock the gear off. I got the one gear and didn't get the nose and it doubled back in there and the strut on it came up through the floor.

JOHN LONG: So he got hurt when he hit the ground?

WILLIAM FASKING: He didn't sit down. He was still there and the fly absorber on the nose wheel come up through the floor and hit him on the back. There he laid all sprawled out. It's my fault he said, it's my fault.

JOHN LONG: At least he was honest about it. Why did he say not to land there?

WILLIAM FASKING: The big field, he saw a gunfire out of the corner of it. That's the one that had got that other glider that was sitting there, but then there wasn't no action when I started in there, and I didn't see any pill box but he must have saw it fire and he said any place but there.

I went on the other side of it and there were more gliders crashed in there. There wasn't no room to land.

JOHN LONG: That narrative I read said that instead of you making a 280 degree turn you did an about face and then did a 90 degree.

WILLIAM FASKING: Well, you studied all that stuff before you went in. You had a picture of that in your mind. The only thing about it, you couldn't tell the height of the trees and they said they weren't, I think maybe more than 30 feet high or something like that. They were way higher than that.

JOHN LONG: What about the hedgerows? Everybody talks about the hedgerows.

WILLIAM FASKING: Well of course in with the trees were the hedgerows.

JOHN LONG: Did they tell you that there was going to be hedgerow problems?

WILLIAM FASKING: Oh yeah, we had photographs to study.

JOHN LONG: As best you can tell me, where did you land that glider the first time you went into Normandy? Was it close to St. Mere-Eglise?

WILLIAM FASKING: Oh St. Mere-Eglise, I think I saw somewhere it was 6.5 kilometers south of St. Mere-Eglise.

JOHN LONG: And you had the paratroopers in there?

WILLIAM FASKING: I had 13 guys, yeah.

JOHN LONG: Yeah, but they weren't jumping out were they?

WILLIAM FASKING: If they were jumpers they would have been raising hell.

JOHN LONG: What I am getting at, I was right there, in June. There is a village called Graignes. Also there was this St. Mere-Eglise where the paratrooper got hung on the church.

WILLIAM FASKING: Well yes, St. Mere-Eglise is. Yup, you are right.

JOHN LONG: Which beach did you guys fly over?

WILLIAM FASKING: Utah was the one with the high cliff on it and then you would just turn inlet like that and the other one Utah and what was the other one? I can't think of it.

JOHN LONG: Omaha. Omaha is the one that had the big cliffs.

WILLIAM FASKING: Okay, Omaha is the one and Utah.

JOHN LONG: It was like a regular beach out there I guess.

WILLIAM FASKING: There was a beach on the front of the other one too for that matter. In fact it would have been better off if they hadn't had because the first two waves of the Third Infantry, I think it was the Third Infantry, the first two waves didn't make it.

JOHN LONG: The fellow told me, I talked to one guy who was in the fifth wave and he said the first two, like you said, didn't make it, just a few of the third, and then some of the forth, and about half of his fifth wave.

WILLIAM FASKING: You know there is another thing here. Those guys came off of those landing ships and there were holes out there and a lot of them guys fell in them holes and had to shed their hardware to save themselves.

JOHN LONG: Yeah, they couldn't swim with that heavy stuff.

WILLIAM FASKING: When we met up with them some of those guys were without their equipment and they were waiting for us.

Bradford C. Freeman Interview Continued

Bradford C. Freeman was a paratrooper that landed behind enemy lines of Utah Beach in the early morning hours of D-Day.

BRADFORD FREEMAN: We went flying through the Gergen Jersey Islands. That is what they told me, I didn't know nothing about it. Anyway, when we first flew over the Gergens and the Jersey Islands that's when we knowed we was there. We went in.

We was supposed to jump at a certain place. Well, the cloud come through and dispersed our airplanes and we didn't know where, and we didn't come no where close to the jump field.

If we had of none of us would have been here because they had that place surrounded. They could flood it and they had it zeroed in. They knowed we were coming.

They even asked some of the prisoners they took how come we were a day late.

My squad leader of the mortars was from Oregon. There was one of the Germans captured went to school with him out there in Oregon and he asked him said what the hell you doing here and he said Hitler called us home.

JOHN LONG: That was in the movie *Band of Brothers*.

BRADFORD FREEMAN: Yeah, the boy lives in Salem Oregon now.

JOHN LONG: Is it true that that guy killed those POW's like shown in the movie?

BRADFORD FREEMAN: I wouldn't say. I didn't see it. I heard it. That's whenever that passed on. He became a company commander.

JOHN LONG: When you say you jumped in, did ya'll land in a place that was, if I understand it was better than if you had jumped in your regular drop zone because they had flooded that area?

Where you finally wound up landing, it wasn't where you were supposed to land but if you had landed where you were supposed to land it would have been surrounded by Germans more.

BRADFORD FREEMAN: That's what they say.

JOHN LONG: What was the first objective that you can recall after you landed? Was there a specific town? St. Lo was up in there somewhere.

BRADFORD FREEMAN: First, we were trying to assemble or trying to get together. That was our objective right then was trying to get together and I got with a Sergeant. He was in E-Company and in the 2nd Platoon but he was the 1st platoon leader. I was in the 4th squad.

He was from St. Louis. His name was Grant and the boy told me before that, he was the only one I ever had that sort of got in to me, he told me to call him Ulysses S. Grant, and I did.

Well he told me on no uncertain terms I should call him Sergeant Grant, nothing else. Not sarge, not sergeant, but Sergeant Grant when I spoke to him. He is the fellow I got behind.

JOHN LONG: Did ya'll use those crickets?

BRADFORD FREEMAN: Yes sir.

JOHN LONG: How scattered were the men when ya'll landed; was it like a big radius or were you all in close proximity?

BRADFORD FREEMAN: They said they were scattered from Normandy to Paris. Some went all the way to Paris. Now, that is hearsay. That's a pretty big spot. You see, our company commander, the company fellow, his plane went down and killed all of them.

They didn't find it till 1968 they tell me and the people were there. I think I saw that plane go down behind the woods but I wouldn't say. The field I landed in was like that out there.

There was five pretty white-faced cows, nobody around. They tell me I was in the first three planes, but I don't know. That's all hearsay.

JOHN LONG: You can guarantee you were there early though?

BRADFORD FREEMAN: Yes, sir. I was early so I saw a plane come over and a fellow come down. I went down there and saw it was my buddy.

He broke his leg. He was Lewis Lampas, from Atlanta Georgia. He worked for the light and power over there. I put him in a thicket, a briar thicket, took his shoe and put it off down there in the woods. I told him you can take care of things here.

He landed right beside the road sort of. I said you can take care of things here. I said well I got to go; we got business to tend to somewhere else. So he gave me a good cussing.

JOHN LONG: For leaving him? I imagine he did say something to you about that.

BRADFORD FREEMAN: But that was alright. He was a good soldier after that, but it did, it broke his leg.

117

JOHN LONG: Do you remember any other instances that kind of like stands out that you would like to tell us about. Just kind of reminisce a little bit about your experiences during that point in time right shortly after the jump, the first jump and landing out there where the perfect cattle were.

BRADFORD FREEMAN: Well we got gathered up at St. Mere-Eglise. That's where it took off from.

JOHN LONG: So when you landed ya'll were up near St. Mere-Eglise?

BRADFORD FREEMAN: Yes.

JOHN LONG: You know that is where the paratrooper got hung up on the steeple.

BRADFORD FREEMAN: Yes sir. That's a picture right there of the window in that church. My granddaughter went over there. She married a boy that his Daddy was a missionary so she took the pictures and she put that together and gave it to me.

JOHN LONG: That's inside the church. That disk that I gave you my wife took the same pictures, inside the church and the steeple outside St. Mere-Eglise. About how far did ya'll land from, in miles, from the town?

BRADFORD FREEMAN: I would say about two maybe three, not very far. We were there by good daylight. Of course, it wasn't dark no time much over there anyway. It was light at 11 o'clock.

JOHN LONG: For some reason or another it stays light late at night over there right in that part of the world. My wife even remarked on that when we were there this summer. About how many guys formed up with the crickets and so forth?

BRADFORD FREEMAN: Well, we finally got a pretty good bunch. There was 13 that took care of the guns and the rest of us guarded the roads, stopped the traffic. Nobody helped the ones that could be going. None of the Germans could get there, because they were taken care of before they could get there.

JOHN LONG: From St. Mere-Eglise, from there what direction did ya'll go, south or north?

BRADFORD FREEMAN: I really don't know. But you know them Germans they changed the road signs. Some of them had us going; of course we would stop there and argue about it, they would. I didn't say nothing about it. I was always behind; I was never a front man.

JOHN LONG: They weren't paying any attention to your map reading abilities much no way were they?

BRADFORD FREEMAN: Not too much.

Earnest Wallace Interview Continued

 I asked Earnest Wallace to tell me about his jump into Normandy.

EARNEST WALLACE: Well we jumped in Normandy, supposed to jump at 300 feet, but when they got to shooting at us, you know I couldn't wait to get there and I looked down and saw all them ships and I didn't know there were that many ships in the world.

In fact I didn't know what it was. I asked somebody what it was and they said that's ships going in the English Channel to France, and so when we hit the coast I thought it was popcorn popping but it was bullets going through.

JOHN LONG: That pilot dumped you then?

EARNEST WALLACE: Well yeah, I wanted out of that plane and my pilot had done the right thing and he was one of the few that did do the right thing. Most of them would lead the plane up and went up. I am sure I jumped at 300 feet.

JOHN LONG: He went down lower huh?

EARNEST WALLACE: See, the tracers…when they shot them over the top of me in Normandy I could smell where the tracers went through that line of shooting. All I could see was tracers.

JOHN LONG: Was that at nighttime?

EARNEST WALLACE: Oh yeah. I cut my chute off at 1:20 D-Day morning and the beach invasion wasn't until 6:00.

JOHN LONG: You all jumped behind the lines.

EARNEST WALLACE: We were behind the lines during the whole war. Three miles to 100 miles. When we left Bastogne we were behind the lines there.

JOHN LONG: Did you jump anywhere around that town Graignes? Where did you jump into Normandy?

EARNEST WALLACE: Right out of St. Mere-Eglise.

JOHN LONG: That's where that guy got hung up on the…

EARNEST WALLACE: That's right, on the church steeple. The 82nd was supposed to jump there so the 101st and the 82nd was all there. I was nine miles from my jump zone, nine miles. Now, you want me to talk about Normandy?

JOHN LONG: Yeah.

EARNEST WALLACE: Coming down out of the plane I could see the highway. It looked like water, but with all the equipment on me, and I couldn't collapse that chute, and I knew I was going to hit water and it frightened me pretty good, but I went under the power line beside the highway and my chute went over the power line, my head was in the ditch beside the highway, my feet was right towards the highway with my chute on top of me.

You talk about a mess. That was a mess. But somehow, I don't remember too much about how I got out, but I had a dagger strapped to my leg and I finally got my dagger out and I think I cut myself loose.

Finally I got up and I heard somebody coming down the highway and we had these little brown crickets and I clicked it and he answered me and it was my supply sergeant, so me and him went…I jumped with a camera in behind my reserve chute.

We went across this pasture, I guess it was at least a block before you got into town, maybe more, and I saw a little horse and I took the camera out and took a picture. I knew it was black, you know, dark, and when I got into St. Mere-Eglise the first thing I saw was a German sitting with his head against a telephone post and a knife, and I saw people climbing telephone poles, and I said this is the 82nd doing this.

That was their mission, to dig a hole and cut the cable and cut the wires up there. Then I finally got with Tom, I don't know what, it was before daylight. We were moving down this street. I don't guess we knew where we was going but there was an officer with us, a lieutenant.

And here came a horse, one horse with a two-wheeled buggy, and when he came around, him and the driver, we captured them, and that officer that was with us, I guessed that we was trying to question him and he spit in his face and Tom was standing there, I was standing back a little ways and Tom emptied his M1 in him and that was it.

JOHN LONG: Because the guy spit in the officers face? So, when you got there your shoe got tangled up in a power line, you were upside down, you had to cut yourself loose, right?

EARNEST WALLACE: I don't remember exactly if I cut myself loose or not, but I got out of that. See I was in a mess with all that chute on me. My head was in a ditch and I couldn't get up to save my life.

JOHN LONG: Somebody else may have got you out.

EARNEST WALLACE: I was by myself.

JOHN LONG: What was the idea of giving you a camera?

EARNEST WALLACE: One of the officers had a 48 hour pass to London and he didn't have much money and he offered to sell me the film and the camera. I don't remember how much I paid him for it but I bought it.

JOHN LONG: So he needed something to go to town on and he sold you the camera?

EARNEST WALLACE: I put the strap around my neck and put the camera under my reserve chute. I wasn't supposed to do that.

JOHN LONG: I was wandering that. What was the purpose of a camera on a paratrooper jumping in the middle of the night?

EARNEST WALLACE: When we got back to England from Normandy I took it to London to the Stars and Stripes and they developed that film and I had some pretty good pictures. I still had some, but I don't remember where they at now. That horse that I took there at St. Mere-Eglise, you could see that horse in that picture and it was black as everything. No light anywhere. It was cloudy you know.

JOHN LONG: Were you briefed that you were going to be dropped into St. Mere-Eglise?

EARNEST WALLACE: We had a drop zone. The pathfinders were going in first and setting up a radar. Well, our plane was set down in the channel, right at the beach and we didn't have….my pilot, didn't have a radar and that is why everyone jumped around St. Mere-Eglise, the 82nd, the 101st.

JOHN LONG: And you already said you were several miles off your jump zone.

EARNEST WALLACE: Nine miles. Right at the breaking of day somebody told me that they wanted to…our mission was a bridge there and we was to capture the town and save the bridge for the British.

Well, when I got there they had already captured a German. A few of them men went down there and captured the town and saved the bridge, but when I got down there, it was somewhere around noon or something, but I could see

Omaha from where I was standing and all I could see was all those dead men out on the beach, and it looked awful.

That's when I prayed to God that I jumped.

JOHN LONG: So you and Tom stayed together during that period of time?

EARNEST WALLACE: Yeah. We were together during the whole war. That's the reason they called us those damn rebels from North Carolina.

JOHN LONG: Talk some more about Normandy.

EARNEST WALLACE: The first time we got our F Company together we moved down the highway, we had a stone wall down there with two machine guns, and we were to go down there and capture the guns, or kill them or whatever.

We was going down that, not a highway, but a road. It was paved, but we got to this house sitting up a little on a hill and a German ran out from behind the house and threw a hand grenade down the driveway.

One of them troopers picked it up and threw it back. Of course it went off over there and I jumped the ditch and we ran around beside the house and covered the back, and I don't know what the rest of them done on the other side of the house, but there were three Germans at that place.

Two of them took off and run in the house but the third one didn't quite make it you know.

There was a man and his wife and a little girl. I didn't see the little girl but I saw and talked to the man, or tried to, but years later that little girl grew up and had a son and he wanted to know who that soldier was that captured them two Germans in his house, and the man that wrote the book about the Fox Company told him to call me, and he called me.

That boy's mother grew up and had that son and he was in the Airborne in the French Army. We sent letters and pictures back to him.

JOHN LONG: Now this was French? The family was French?

EARNEST WALLACE: Oh yeah. We moved back to the coast. We were going to go back to England, and all at once we took off for Carentan through them hedgerows, and that was terrible.

The first morning we were fighting the German paratroopers that were there. They were defending Carentan and we beat the mud out of them, I guarantee you that. Of course they killed a whole lot of our people, and we killed a whole lot of them.

We finally captured Carentan but then they brought the tanks, the airplanes and the artillery in on us and they were trying to take it back; that was a very, very important job to take and hold Carentan.

There were four highways there right into Carentan. We held on until the tanks cleared off of Omaha and come there and relieved us.

JOHN LONG: Tell us about the hedgerows. One thing I have never really fully….

EARNEST WALLACE: Let me tell you something…they are hundreds of years old. The way I figure it they put rocks up and down there and put dirt on top of them and then planted hedges.

Some of them was that big around and as tall as this house and tanks couldn't even go through them.

That was a pasture and a fence for the cows and it had a gate up there on each one. Well, the Germans, they came out of them hedgerows just a flying.

They had never fought anybody that fought back you see before the invasion. Everybody took off and gave up. They hadn't fought anybody.

JOHN LONG: My question was about the hedgerows was that it presented a very difficult problem for the invasion forces but it didn't look to me that ya'll were prepared for the hedgerow problem.

EARNEST WALLACE: No, we wasn't prepared. I don't know, that was a crazy, wild bunch of people in 1st Cavalry, I tell you. You wouldn't believe what went on; you would have just had to have seen it.

That bunch that invaded France on D-Day morning, they never got to bomb anything. They were ready. We went back to England and got on the plane twice to jump ahead of Patton, but every time we got on the plane Patton had done passed where we were going to jump.

JOHN LONG: He was rolling wasn't he?

Harold Powers Interview Continued

Harold Powers was a paratrooper that was captured and remained a prisoner of war for the duration of the war.

I asked him to describe his D-Day jump and his capture.

HAROLD POWERS: I don't know the name of the town where we jumped. It wasn't a town; it was a church and a little village at a crossroads. That is where we jumped and landed out in a little ole pasture there. The people that jumped in front of me ended up in the courtyard where there was Germans and got killed right away.

JOHN LONG: Is that the place where the fellow got hung up on the church steeple?

HAROLD POWERS: No, that was St. Mere-Eglise. Of us jumping there where we did, I only know of about five that survived of my jump.

JOHN LONG: How many was in that group?

HAROLD POWERS: Five out of 14 survived that I knew of. There might have been one wounded of that. The company first sergeant and also the captain jumped with us and they got killed.

JOHN LONG: Do you remember what your specific mission was for that particular group?

HAROLD POWERS: That particular group was supposed to be in reserve and jump with the General and set up headquarters and protect it; and the regiment was to take

Carentan, the town there that had the locks where the river came in and emptied into the ocean there. They had locks there.

JOHN LONG: We were there back in June of this year and we went to Graignes, and that is where the worse drop was, where they dropped fellows in the swamp.

HAROLD POWERS: Oh yeah, that happened, because as I say, it was sort of panic with the pilots because they just strung them out everywhere. Some of them just drown and things like that I'm sure.

JOHN LONG: We spent two nights in St. Lo and Carentan is about half way between there and Cherbourg. That was the port city up on the other end. Do you remember specifically in relation to the landings in the landing craft and ya'll was behind that in relation to D-Day itself, when were you jumping out?

HAROLD POWERS: We jumped out about one or two o'clock in the morning on June the 6th and got captured later that afternoon.

JOHN LONG: Before you got captured do you recall any instances of what happened, the hedgerows and that sort of thing?

HAROLD POWERS: We jumped and after I got out of my chute and got with another fellow we had a little activity there with the Germans of course, and then when it got daylight we circled to the back of the church and was going around to where we could hear gunfire.

It was 30 caliber machine guns shooting, and we figured that is where the rest of the troops were. We didn't know that we were the only plane load that jumped right there. It was about 17 miles from the drop zone.

JOHN LONG: It was that far off?

HAROLD POWERS: The way you jump is, the pilot turns on the red light, you stand up and check your chutes and all that stuff and then they press the green light when it's time to jump.

JOHN LONG: Well, can you think of anything else you would like to say about that period of time right in there when you jumped?

HAROLD POWERS: Yeah, going out to where we heard the gunfire thinking it was our troops over there. Because we had an idea that there was nobody else much around because when we jumped, when I jumped I looked up and there was not a soul coming out of the other planes that came over and I knew something was wrong.

JOHN LONG: You knew you were supposed to be in a crowd and you weren't.

HAROLD POWERS: They was supposed to be everywhere around. We went up and down the hedgerow and wandered back to pretty close to where that gunfire was and picked up another person and while we were there he told us that our platoon sergeant had gotten killed and that the Germans had our guns that was packed into a big chute and dropped, and they recovered that.

We three got together and was going to see if we could find anybody else and got away from that area because we were pretty close. We got one shot at us and we decided to go down the hedgerow and while we were about half way down the road Kirby got killed. That is one of the people that was with me, and we continued on after Kirby got killed and we ran into three more people, and one of those was a general's interpreter or translator.

JOHN LONG: The one that was on the plane with you?

HAROLD POWERS: Yeah. We were strung out. You looked for where they were coming from. In other words go in a straight line across there and you try to wander back up to see if there were any more of the troops.

JOHN LONG: Did y'all use the crickets?

HAROLD POWERS: Oh yeah. You ever seen one? I got one in there in the other room.

JOHN LONG: The one you got is not the same one they gave you to jump with is it?

HAROLD POWERS: No, No. The Germans got that one, but it's just like it. It was just like the one we used when I found this other fellow. He clicked his and I clicked mine and there he was hid right in the hedgerow.

He got out of there and he joined us and that's when we proceeded to look for other soldiers going in a different direction from where all the gunfire was coming from.

JOHN LONG: You said you jumped kind of in the early morning hours before daylight, when you was finding these fellows, like you found the interpreter that was with you on the plane, was it still dark?

HAROLD POWERS: No, this was about 11 or 12 o'clock.

JOHN LONG: What about the action. Was there was sort of firing going on and you find out you were surrounded?

HAROLD POWERS: No, no. They just surrounded us and we didn't know it and even though we had somebody as a lookout there but we was sort of in a low place in a ditch like and he was up on level ground.

JOHN LONG: Now, the General's interrupter, was he a French speaking fellow or a German?

HAROLD POWERS: German.

JOHN LONG: He kind of like told you what was going on?

HAROLD POWERS: Yeah, when they asked us to surrender, he said they got us surrounded and what have you. We had no choice and when we stood up and I looked back over through the hedgerow they had guns right in the back of us and in front of us.

JOHN LONG: They told you the truth about being surrounded?

HAROLD POWERS: Yeah

JOHN LONG: You are the first person that I have interviewed that was a POW. The rest of them never said anything about being a POW.

HAROLD POWERS: They probably wasn't.

JOHN LONG: Tell us a little about that experience, about being a POW, where you were taken and how you were treated and just tell us the best you can about that.

HAROLD POWERS: After we got captured they took us to a place there on Normandy that we called Starvation Hill. We went without food for about a week there and they started moving us back.

We moved and kept moving until we were completely out of the area. They put us on the train and carried us up near Paris and then they decided to talk to us and see what we knew and everything and interrogate us.

A lot of us they shocked. They called it (shocktraceous) because we didn't know how to pronounce it I suppose. It was in that area that they interrogated us, and when they brought me in there they said that fellow we just interviewed, is he crazy or something another.

He wasn't giving them anything you know, no information, but they got us in groups that were captured together. When they got me in there they wanted to know where we came

132

from and all that sort of stuff you know, where did we fly out of and I said I don't know.

They questioned me some more about that. They said well who does know and I said ya'll killed him. I said you killed the one, our leader, just like you a lieutenant and these other people you are their leader.

They got disgusted with not knowing. I said I am just a private, so they let me go and from there we went to Paris and caught a train out of there back into Germany to camps to get the dog tags that the prisoners got, and kept moving back until we got to an English prison camp.

We stayed there until September and they moved us out from there, those that were privates to work camps. I ended up then in Czechoslovakia, in a coal mine area. I first started out digging out bomb shelters and then it got so cold we couldn't take that, Americans couldn't and they let us go into the coal mines and took the Russians out to do that outside labor.

There were glass factories there and other places the boys worked. Some was sent to sugar farms to get sugar beets and things like that. We stayed there. I was one of the lucky ones. I drew something similar to an engineer that went around from shaft to shaft in the coal mine just picking out places where to bore new holes to start a new shaft and things like that.

But the thing about it was I fared better than most of the boys with me because he gave me half of his food that he had for breakfast. When he came in we would eat something.

JOHN LONG: You say we, who were the we?

HAROLD POWERS: Me and the German that I was working with. He would share his food with me. The

133

German worker there understood that the war was coming to an end there and stuff like that.

JOHN LONG: Did y'all kind of like, not necessarily become friends but become acquaintances?

HAROLD POWERS: Oh yeah.

JOHN LONG: Did you ever correspond after the war?

HAROLD POWERS: Couldn't. Never did get his address and then he ended up in the Russian area when they divided up the country.

JOHN LONG: Do you have any recollections about what towns you were in Germany after they put you on that train in Paris and carried you back?

HAROLD POWERS: Back to an industrial area. Yeah, we ended up in the Sudetenland. I know you have heard of that, which was Germany in World War I and they took it from them and made Czechoslovakia via other people in there with them. They had given up during the war with Hitler, well they didn't actually start no war, they just let him move right in.

JOHN LONG: Did you recall about where the English camp was?

HAROLD POWERS: It was pretty close to Berlin. Not too far back. Man, they know how to run a prison camp, the English. There were German guards but the English took it over and handled everything. Of course, they had been in prison for two or three years probably, some of them.

JOHN LONG: In my training, they told me if you got captured, the only thing you had to give them was your name, rank, and serial number. If you tried that on them, they didn't like that did they?

HAROLD POWERS: Well, that is what we gave them to start with but they kept quizzing us. I said, hey man, I don't know.

Jack Carver Interview Continued

I asked Jack Carver to just give me a picture of what it was like when they actually made the invasion.

JACK CARVER: Well, I didn't go right on the first one. I was right behind them. Anyway, it was getting dark, we were right on the coast, and we were going across the channel where they dropped them out.

JOHN LONG: At that time did you drop paratroopers or did you haul tanks?

JACK CARVER: My first trip, they had done dropped them that first trip there. When I saw the load of the airplane it scared me. We had about ten to twenty-five gallons of gas in that airplane and they had done pushed them Germans back a little bit off the coast, and the CBs I guess, they put us down a steel flat to land on out there in a field somewhere and we landed on that and threw that gas out. That was for all those tanks and everything else.

JOHN LONG: So, you were actually resupplying them with fuel?

JACK CARVER: The General, he was going up through Germany so fast we could hardly keep up with them.

JOHN LONG: Ole Patton it sounds like. Do you remember what area that you went down into France there and supplied the troops; was it near St. Lo, or was it near St. Mere-Eglise, or Pointe Du Hoc or somewhere like that?

JACK CARVER: Well, it was right where the invasion was. I forget the name of that river where they had the invasion, but its right there where it was. We had the 82nd Airborne and the 101st Airborne, all of them to carry over there.

JOHN LONG: The reason I thought about St. Lo and up in there was, I think that is where Patton got his tank supplies and so forth to make that run down through there.

JACK CARVER: It was probably right close to that. It probably was. Let me tell you that first time when we carried that gas over there and they got that gas out while we were throwing them cans out, as we threw them out they had people out there picking them up. At that time we had these fighter planes that flew above us to kind of protect us.

We didn't have no gun in there or nothing. About the time, here comes this P-47 in there with his engines...all that thing is a big ole engine you know. That engine was just shot all to pieces and he came in and he landed in the grass out there right in front of us. We got him and carried him back to England.

He said he bet he was the only one that had crashed landed and got back on the first day.

JOHN LONG: He landed in the right spot, didn't he?

JACK CARVER: The right spot. They had P-51s and 47's and P-38s flying above us. See, to drop troopers we didn't fly but 500 feet off the ground, and everybody was shooting at you from the ground.

JOHN LONG: Well, you talking about getting shot at, give us, to the best of your recollection, did you have any close calls that you can think of?

JACK CARVER: Well not right there at that time I didn't, but the next time we had this; I don't know what they call this, but it was later on during the war, and it had this line of airplanes carrying…they were supposed to meet up with the English over there.

They was going one way and we were going in, I think they called it Margaret's Garden or something, that's what they called that project they were doing, but anyway we got out there and we had three airplanes flying; we had one here and one flying on each wing. That's the way they had us lined up to fly.

As far as I could see in front of me, in front of that airplane, you could see airplanes up there where they were flying over and then we got two that go that a way and over there and they would just park.

You could see the black smoke starting, just popping out right all around these airplanes. They were shooting at them you see. I remember, I told this fellow, I said "reckon we ought to turn around and go back?" I just said that to get a laugh about it, I knew we couldn't do that.

Anyway, when we got over there and the paratroopers got out to the jump zone, everybody would jump out and we would have to go turn and head back home. While we were turning there was a big explosion. I just knew it was our airplane.

I knew it was my airplane, or I thought it was. I said I was scared to step back, scared I would fall through a hole. But it wasn't my airplane. I looked outside and the airplane that was flying on my right wing, both his engines were on fire, just smoking and everything.

We watched them and he went down and hit the ground and hit the dirt and they all got out of it. We saw them getting out of the airplane. You know they got back to their outfit. It didn't take long either.

***

So we see that the Airborne landed in farm fields in fragile gliders, or descending in parachutes amid antiaircraft fire. The airborne troops suffered heavy casualties.

In the darkness and confusion of the pre-dawn hours, many units became scattered and disorganized. Some men who landed in flooded areas drowned.

Despite these difficulties, groups of soldiers managed to form up and attack the enemy.

Eugene Meier Interview Continued

We stayed in a barb wire enclosure until about the end of May when we were transferred to the south of England to the embarkation points.

It was unbelievable how many trucks, tanks, halftracks, bulldozers and all that were piled up.

We were enclosed with barbed wire with fences about eight foot high and they were two or three fences separated by four or five feet. That was still with barbed wire. We were literally locked up inside of a prison camp.

The second D-Day we were there the officers were all called in and we were briefed on the invasion; where, what date, what time, who would be involved, what time we would load our landing craft, all the fine minor details, where we would pick our explosives up and all this kind of stuff.

When I was assigned in charge of both Teams A, which was a support team company, I was the officer in charge. I had 23 enlisted men and a combat medic in my landing craft, an LCM.

When we loaded, we sailed on the Princess Maud, which was a coastal steamer, channel steamer, and it anchored off the shore. We loaded on the 5th and unloaded that night. We unloaded because of the storm and we loaded up again the night of the 5th and sailed.

Each one of the men, myself, my 23 enlisted men, each carried a canvas sack on our chest holding eight 2.5 lb blocks of plastic explosives. We had another pack of this, identical pack on our back so each one of us carried 40 lbs. of explosives, 20 on our chest and 20 on our back, along with other special equipment that we were carrying, such as detonators, everything else.

We were 12 miles off shore and we went down the side of the Princess Maud into our landing craft. Now this is in a rough sea. Now, there was only one other on board the landing craft and he was the driver, so the first two men down each grabbed the end of net going down and they kept it taught because the ship was standing still but the landing craft was bobbing up and down in rough water, and if it went up on a wave it moved against the ship the man that was in there he would be trapped between it and be crushed so they kept the line taught so that when a man came down they went directly into the landing craft.

I got down, the landing craft was a high point so I said it was a good time to let go, so I let go of the net and jumped towards the boat and fell about six feet because it was on the way down and I didn't realize it and I had fallen all the way to the bottom.

We went out and took up our waiting positions and the noise was intolerable.

We were 12 miles out and all the naval vessels were firing their weapons. We had rockets going in overhead. That was the first time I had seen a military rocket being fired anyway, and all sorts of things.

A lot of the artillery units had their guns set up in the bottom of the landing craft and they were firing, so the noise, the smoke, the smell and everything it was unbelievable.

Our battalion was split up from the trip to England over. Some of the men went on the Princess Maud, which I was one of them. The big majority loaded on LCTs, and they towed their landing craft behind them and because of the high waters they launched them into the landing craft and they were tossed about like corks in the rough sea, and roughly 60 to 70% of them got sick somewhere in that 12 miles trip.

They said there was nothing for them to be standing ankle deep in the previous night's meal. We landed, we did our job.

We stayed on the beach four or five days, I think, I am not exactly sure. At that point we moved inland and after two days of waiting for our trucks and our basic equipment to come into us we headed north into France headed for Paris.

***

Seasickness; a Major Enemy

Walter Cronkite interviewed General Eisenhower about seasickness on D-Day.

CRONKITE: I have heard some of your subordinate commanders say that the greatest enemy they faced on D-Day was seasickness.

EISENHOWER: Well, I think by and large that was true..... It was serious of course. Some of the men took so much Dramamine that they got sleepy. You almost had to duck them in water to wake them up.

CRONKITE: Some of the men were actually in small landing craft for several hours before landing?

EISENHOWER: Oh, yes. As a matter of fact, as some of our second waves came up close to shore, Omaha beach was so jammed, because the troops couldn't get off the beach, there was no place for the boats to come in. They began to circle out in the water, and someone described them as "a herd of milling cattle". They stayed out there, some of them, for two hours, just rocking and chasing around in a circle. They had to keep moving. Otherwise, they would have made themselves too attractive as targets.

It was terrible.

Ivy Agee Interview Continued

JOHN LONG: You were in the first wave.

IVY AGEE: Yeah, I was in the first wave.

JOHN LONG: Tell us about the actual landing, when you got off the ship and how many was on your crew and how many vehicles got off. And tell me about your landing craft.

IVY AGEE: The landing craft, it was a flat boat but the front of it would drop down so whoever was on it could get off real fast and not have to climb over the side of it, so we were lucky that we had a boat that we could get off of real quick and not have to stay in the same place for so long, so that was real good and did a lot of good too. Did a lot of good. I was the only vehicle that made it off except a 6 by 6 truck. The rest of them were destroyed, so when I got on base I had to leave it.

JOHN LONG: Tell us about getting on the beach.

IVY AGEE: I had to leave my jeep and come back later for it because the fire was so heavy. I couldn't stay there unless I got killed.

141

When I came off my jeep I was steering under here and tiptoeing as far as I could tiptoe out of the water, my nose just barely out of the water. I came on out and never did stop. You know a lot of times you will stall a little bit. It never did stop; it came out just as pretty.

JOHN LONG: Did you have any other equipment on the landing craft besides the jeep?

IVY AGEE: No.

JOHN LONG: One question that popped in my mind, you came in on Omaha Beach. Were you where you could see those cliffs where the rangers...

IVY AGEE: Oh yes, I could see those cliffs, yeah, cause we were under those cliffs. They opened up and out where we were coming on the beach. That's the reason I had to crawl across these two dead soldiers was to get behind those walls for some protection.

JOHN LONG: When you got on the beach and got up to the higher ground, there was one gentleman that said they came around and got some of them Germans that was sniping? Were you involved in that?

IVY AGEE: Where I was going there were a lot of snipers up in trees. You couldn't see them, they were behind the limbs or leaves and would hide themselves and you couldn't tell until they shot at you and you heard the guns go off.

JOHN LONG: A lot was said about the hedgerows, they were hiding in the hedgerows.

IVY AGEE: Those hedgerows were something. A tank couldn't go through those hedgerows in some places, it was so thick and all it would just stop the tank. It would just stop the tank, those hedgerows would and after they got one hole open through there they were okay.

After we got on top of this bluff I remember seeing a lot of Germans dead. I think that was probably shells from the aircraft.

After that was destroyed it was just easy then. We could just do anything then we wanted to.

JOHN LONG: Once you got over the hump so to speak...

IVY AGEE: After we got over the hump we were okay.

James L. Springer Interview Continued

 We didn't know it was D-Day or when it was going to be. We came back up the English Channel and parked next to a battleship.

All that day, at D-Day this battleship was shooting those 16 gauge cannons over on the shore.

On D-Day the sky was just black with airplanes going over. It was quite a sight.

On D-Day plus 1 we climbed down a rope from the ship to the landing craft and we went close to France on Omaha Beach and got off the landing craft. Water was about chest deep.

JOHN LONG: What did you do when you got out of the water and got to the beach?

JAMES SPRINGER: I don't actually remember. I was too concerned about getting on the beach.

JOHN LONG: What's your first recollection after you landed?

JAMES SPRINGER: Jumping off in that water and seeing all the barricades the Germans had put in the water. We got on the beach; I think we stayed on the beach overnight.

The next day we marched into France and started the combat.

JOHN LONG: What's your first memory of that?

JAMES SPRINGER: We knew there were a bunch of Germans up there in that next area and I was placing my men along the hedgerow and I told one guy to get down here and as soon as he got down there the sniper fire got him. It came out the back of his head, brains and everything pouring out the back of his head. I still feel I was responsible.

JOHN LONG: You weren't anywhere around St. Lo or that area, I don't believe.

JAMES SPRINGER: I got shot in the ear; it went through my ear and out the back. We were in France after a couple days I guess, doing our usual thing of trying to liberate the Germans and snipers were still on the beach and they asked our squadron to go and hunt snipers so we went back to the beach area and was getting ready to go try to find them and a sniper opened up on us and shot me.

JOHN LONG: Did you get medical attention? Did they carry you back to the…

JAMES SPRINGER: Back there, waiting there at the coast and there were fishing boats. We went to England. I stayed in the hospital for six weeks while my shot was healing and I went back to France and joined another outfit, which was the 38th Infantry.

I reported to the First Sergeant. As soon as I got there he said I was proud of you at that time. You were over there as a Staff Sergeant and you had a squad of people, soldiers. The first thing he said was to take your squad and go down in the field and do some marching.

I wasn't very good at that cause that is not the kind of training I had. So I came back up there. The next morning we started advancing from hedgerow to hedgerow. There is a lot of misconception about what a hedge row is.

JOHN LONG: Tell us about the hedgerows.

JAMES SPRINGER: Well, hedgerows, when they are clearing their land they take all the rocks and everything and put it on the edge of the field and the vines would grow up through the hedgerow. Some of them would be ten feet tall.

JOHN LONG: How did you get through the hedgerows?

JAMES SPRINGER: Climbed over them. We could see the Germans then.

JOHN LONG: After you had been there a while they made you a sergeant, is that correct?

JAMES SPRINGER: Yeah.

JOHN LONG: Then where did you go inland from there? Do you recall any places that you went?

JAMES SPRINGER: We went through St. Lo. Later we went down to Brest France, and my squad was at a bridge across the river at Brest. We were on the bridge going into Brest. They said you are not supposed to be on that bridge, we are not going in there until tomorrow.

JOHN LONG: So you were ahead of them so far, a day ahead of them? So what happened then?

JAMES SPRINGER: We went back over on the land and dug in again, foxholes for the night. That night the Germans started shelling. One of the guys was regular Army. He got killed by a shell in a foxhole.

JOHN LONG: Did you continue on into Germany? Did you stay with the outfit all the way across the Rhine?

JAMES SPRINGER: No. We were somewhere outside of Brest. We started on the mortar shells and tried to get to where ---- were and after the mortar bombardment ---

JOHN LONG: They went off in the air?

JAMES SPRINGER: Yeah and everybody dug in. We had the first hot meal that we had had and they was serving it and started them shells bursting in the air. As soon as they did that I dived for my ----- and got it on top of me. That was the second time. Shrapnel went through my chest and into my lung and broke my arm.

JOHN LONG: That came from the air bursts; the shrapnel?

JAMES SPRINGER: That's right.

JOHN LONG: I guess that was enough to kind of lay you low for a while.

JAMES SPRINGER: Yeah. The medic came and got me on a stretcher and was taking me down to the First Aid Station. He said that hole is too big and you losing too much blood, I am going to have to sew it up, so he put me down on the ground and sewed up that hole and took me on to the field hospital. I don't know whether it was that day or some other day later they operated on me in the Field Hospital; German captives or orderlies at the hospital.

JOHN LONG: Did you kind of keep an eye on them while you were in there?

JAMES SPRINGER: Yeah. On the way back from the hospital we had a loss of our outfit, the sergeant beside me said you better take that P38 that's all you got. I got it off a gentleman.

JOHN LONG: Do you have another account that comes to mind?

JAMES SPRINGER: From there I went back to England again after I was operated on in the Field Hospital and they told me I was unconscious for three days and the guys who operated on me was standing by my side when I woke up. He was telling me what he did, and that I was going to be alright.

So then they put me on a C47 airplane and sent me back over to England to a hospital over there. I stayed in the hospital there from September 7th until about the 22nd of December and got on a Queen Mary and came back to the states.

[I saw that Mr. Springer was growing weaker.]

JOHN LONG: That's some good stories. Let's kind of wind it down because I don't want to overdo it….

JAMES SPRINGER: I remember one time the Germans had a field, had control of a field and we started going down the high grass in the field and about half way through the field there was a canal, we didn't know it was there when we started the battle. Bullets were going over our heads…. we got down in the canal and waded….

JOHN LONG: I think we have imposed long enough. That is great. Let's end the tape here.

Joe Johnson Interview Continued

I was just amazed to see that many ships there. I didn't know the United States and the allied countries had that many ships. I had never seen as many ships in my life since I've been living.

The Germans had sunk so many of them until all you could see was a mast out of the water; the mast pole and that LST Captain just had to maneuver himself around there to get us to the shore.

JOHN LONG: So he was maneuvering around sunken ships?

JOE JOHNSON: Yeah, sunken ships the Germans had sunk a lot of them. But there were even more there at the beach.

JOHN LONG: Did you ever really decide that you went in on Utah and not Omaha?

JOE JOHNSON: Well after we got up into France for sometime the captain came down and said there was no sign on the beach head so I need to tell you we went in on Omaha Beach Head.

I always thought we went in on Omaha but we didn't go in on Omaha Beach Head. It was several years later I went out to the 14th line Training Wing at Columbus Air Force Base and the Wing Commander had been over there and took some pictures and he said "Joe, reckon you would recognize the beach head where you went in at?" I said "I might be able to"

He started showing some pictures and I said no, no, no, no, no, no. He got up to the Utah Beach Head where the

148

Germans had that big gun there, a 24 inch gun mounted in concrete and I said that's where we went in, yeah.

He said you didn't go in on Omaha you went in on Utah. I didn't know that for years.

JOHN LONG: It is my understanding that Utah Beach was the one on the west side and Omaha was on the east, and there wasn't a marker out there.

JOE JOHNSON: No. There was no markers to tell you what beach you were going in on.

JOHN LONG: According to what I've read about the Utah Beach the beach was about three or four miles wide right in there.

JOE JOHNSON: It was a pretty nice beach.

JOHN LONG: So you went when they were delivering more of the heavier equipment?

JOE JOHNSON: Yeah, they were trying to get those tanks on shore so we could push the Germans back. That's what they were wanting those tanks on shore for.

JOHN LONG: After you got on the beach head what did you see?

JOE JOHNSON: Well, I looked around, and I figured out right then as a young boy that I was in trouble. I wandered why in the world I volunteered to go in the military.

JOHN LONG: Was that about the time you thought back about that prayer you had?

JOE JOHNSON: Yeah, I belonged to the Church of Jesus Christ of the Latter Day Saints and my Daddy was an elder. He held the priesthood. The morning I left he and mama was crying, and he said Joe, I need to give you a father's blessing, so he took me in there on the bed.

I looked around at that beach; saw all that mess, I said Heavenly Father, that blessing my Daddy gave me needs to work. It needs to work, and it did work, I can bear witness to the world, it did work.

JOHN LONG: Yeah, tell us about getting off the beach.

Joe Johnson Beyond the Beach

JOE JOHNSON: Now, Mr. Long, you must remember the French had these hedgerows. They were so thick you couldn't get through those things, a dog or cow couldn't go through them.

They were so thick and sticky and those Germans were in behind there and so we had halftracks. Halftrack is a half truck and a half tank; its got truck wheels on the front and tracks on the back like a tank and it had an M1 on there with four 50 calibers and Patton said he wanted us to saw those hedgerows down and we backed that halftrack up there and we sawed those hedgerows down like a weed eater.

JOHN LONG: If I got a picture right in my mind, this hedgerow was so tough to get through that sometimes even a tank couldn't go through it.

JOE JOHNSON: You could push it. It was green so you could push it over with a tank, but you see the Germans were dug in. As soon as we started firing; they knew what we was trying to do; get rid of those hedgerows so we could see them.

JOHN LONG: So you just mowed them down with …

JOE JOHNSON: Those 450s were all firing at one time and Mr. Long it looked like, every fifth round was a tracer and it looked like every one of them coming out of that barrel was a tracer. It looked like a red water hose.

JOHN LONG: That's a story that I remembered. Tell us about some of the things that happened to you after you got into Normandy and France; and I think your outfit got with Patton.

JOE JOHNSON: We landed with the First Army but Eisenhower didn't want the Germans to know the Third Army had landed. See we landed under the cover of the First Army and then in about a week he announced that the Third Army had landed under the cover of the First Army, but we were with the First Army.

We didn't know that. We thought we were the Third Army going on the beachhead, but history will show that we landed under their cover because Eisenhower did not want the Germans to know Patton was up there. He did not want them to know that. He didn't want them to know the Third Army was there.

JOHN LONG: Tell us about some of your encounters with Patton for example.

JOE JOHNSON: Well let me tell you a little bit. After we left the beachhead we went through St. Lo. Those battleships had turned crossways in the English Channel, I think one of them was the USS Alabama but I'm not sure. I didn't see the names on them, but those 16-inch shells was coming over us and hitting those steel boxes and busting those steel boxes all to pieces. That 16-inch shell weighed 600 pounds. You could see it; it didn't travel too fast. That powder on the back end looked like a tracer, but it didn't have a tracer. That black powder it was red hot in the back.

JOHN LONG: One of the things that I thought was interesting in our first interview, you said Patton saw you and he recognized how young you was and said something to you.

151

JOE JOHNSON: Well, let me tell you what happened. Ms. Roosevelt, if you don't know, bless her heart, she was so ugly. She looked like she had been whooped with an ugly stick, but she was a good woman. I'll tell you a good story about her later on, but anyway, she said to her husband you don't need to let them boys go on the beachhead until they get 21, so the Armed Forces Network said that the president said no one could go on the beachhead until they reached 21, and here I was 19.

I told my sergeant, I said Sarge I could go back home, and he said no you ain't, we'll have to get with Patton. Patton came down there and checked us out and he looked at me and said boy you dry behind the ears, let me feel and see if you dry behind the ears. He said you sure are a young boy. He said I can't let you go, you are trained, I'm going to make a soldier out of you, and buddy he did. He made some soldiers out of us.

JOHN LONG: Tell us about the time that you encountered Patton on the road, and you was guarding this roadway and nobody was supposed to go down it and you warned him about going down it.

JOE JOHNSON: Let me tell you a story before I get there. You must remember we moved pretty fast through Germany. We got the Germans on the run. We stayed right after them. We didn't let them sit down and stop. If they stopped we would run over them. They knew that.

When we got to the Rhine River, we couldn't cross the Rhine River, so Patton called Ike and said Ike I need the combat engineers to put me a bridge across the river. He said, George, I don't have any, and he said well get some from somewhere; that's your job, I need the material to get me across that river, so the combat engineers came out there and put us a pontoon bridge across the Rhine River, and we crossed at 2 o'clock in the morning.

When we crossed we knew that we were in German territory then. That was their real home state and we knew that hell was going to break out at daylight.

When daylight came we had dug in real good and across the river when daylight come four P-47 Thunderbolts came up and they looked at us and went on. Evidently they seen the stars on our equipment. These were American P-47 Thunderbolts, but they went on; they left us alone.

I guess, probably seemed like about an hour four P-51 Mustangs came up, so they looked at us. This one guy on the right wing buddy he peeled up and came upside down and leveled off. I saw the smoke coming out of the wing, I never heard the gun a firing but I knew he was firing on us, so we jumped in the gun placement and he came right on over that gun placement and cut the canvas on the truck that was outside over there.

It was an Army truck, we had canvas on it, you know that, anyway he came over and he fired on us and we jumped in there. He didn't kill any of us and didn't hit none of us except the equipment.

He went on down a little piece and pulled up and turned around and looked back and I told Sergeant Warder, my Sergeant, I said Sergeant, if that guy comes back I am going to knock him down, and he said get him, so when he turned around and came back I had that 40 mm; that 40 mm had clips you put in the hopper and it had nine rounds in that clip. It would fire automatic; you could put it on automatic. That was bad of that American pilot.

We tried to run him off but he wouldn't go. There was 160 of us but there wasn't but one of him so I was trying to save all of us and just kill one guy, so I was aiming at the cockpit but it hit behind the cockpit and that 40 mm, that projector has an explosive thing in it; well I cut the tail off right behind the wing and he didn't have an ejection seat, he just turned over and fell out and hit the ground probably 600-800 feet from us; give or take, I'm not sure, but he was in a field and that P-51 was splattered out there.

It was a brand new P-51 right out the factory. I walked out there and I said Lt. what the hell are you doing firing on us. He said "are you an American?" I said I was at 6 o'clock. He said my heaven's the Air Force is coming, you people are in trouble.

We need to get them word; we need to get them information as soon as y'all cross the river. I said we crossed it through this morning and he said they briefed us in England this morning. The Air Force said that everything on the east side of the Rhine River was duck shoot, that you could kill anybody.

I said well my heavens Lieutenant; I can't get a hold of them; we don't have no way to get a hold of them. That was a tail plane. The other planes come up but we run them off. We were able to run some of those off. We had a good antiaircraft outfit. We was crack shot. We were good. That must have been around 8:30 in the morning give or take.

I guess in about an hour or two hours General Patton came down there. He wanted to be with his men. He wanted to know what was going on. He was excited we had crossed the river and he came down there and our company commander, he was from Boston, Mass., and he said "Captain, who shot that airplane down." He said Sergeant Warder who shot it down and he came over there and said Sergeant Warder who shot that airplane down? He said Private First Class Johnson, and I was just a shaking. I was scared to death. He said soldier why did you shoot that plane down and I said "sir, he fired on us twice." He said "well, I would have kicked your butt if you hadn't knocked him down. I felt relieved then. I quit shaking.

JOHN LONG: What about that part about guarding the road that he wanted to go down?

JOE JOHNSON: After we crossed the Rhine River, you know the Germans had a lot of those roads mined, and so Sergeant Warder, the Platoon Sergeant said "Joe take these horses and put them across there and don't let nobody down this road. This road is mined and we can't let nobody down there. I turned all the water trucks and the ammo trucks back and wouldn't let nobody go.

JOHN LONG: So the reason was that the Germans had put mines….

JOE JOHNSON: Yeah, that road was mined. That's the reason the horse was put across there. I turned all the traffic back. In a little bit I heard this jeep coming and I looked. He wore a silver helmet that had pearl pistols on each side and so that silver helmet came around the windshield and I said "oh lord, that's the ole man."

I stopped the driver and I said "driver, you can't go down this road." General Patton said "the hell you say." I said, "General, you can't go down this road. This road is mined." He said "well, who told you I can't go." I said my company commander said nobody go down this road.

General Patton said I am going to give you an order to give me an order to let me go down this road and they can't bother you. So I pulled the horses back and I say "go ahead General."

He went on down the road, and I guess I forgot about him being down there because I was watching those P-51s knock those ME109, they was having a dogfight and I got interested in watching those planes having a dogfight and directly I seen this water truck coming by, an old Dodge water truck and I thought it was just somebody coming out so he told the driver pull over there driver I want to see this

155

soldier, so he pulled over there and he said "sonny boy I played hell; that mine blew the axel out from under my jeep but I'm okay, it didn't hurt us." He said I could use a million of you; like you young feller, then said drive on driver.

JOHN LONG: What about your encounter with the Germans, well they weren't actually German they were Polish.

JOE JOHNSON: Well, I need to tell you what happened. We had to go on reconnaissance. You were assigned every so often in your squadron or your unit to go on reconnaissance. We would go behind enemy lines to draw fire to find out where they were at and who was where. You know what reconnaissance is; to find out what the enemy is doing, if you could feel them out.

It's a scary time in your life. If you step on a stick and it breaks your hair will push the helmet right off your head.

Anyway, that morning I was to go on patrol and so the captain came down there and said Sergeant Warder, you see those two big buildings down in that little town? We were up on a high hill then. We were up on a high place. We always tried to get the high place, because if you was on a high place you could see better. You had an advantage if you got on a high hill.

So we were up there and the captain said Warder you got to check them buildings out down there. Warder came to me and he said well Joe its time for you to go on reconnaissance, y'all got to go down there and check out that building. I want a report on it so go down there and see what's in there.

I had a boy from North Carolina, whose name was Freddy. He had never brushed his teeth. They were gold as they could be. Freddy was sick that morning and couldn't go with me so I told Sergeant Warder that I'll go by myself and he said "Joe, you don't need to do that by yourself" and I said "well you got the guns traced on me. You got your looking binoculars, you can follow me down there," and he said, "well Joe, I don't want you to go by yourself," but I said "I am going to go down there and see what's in there."

I started down that little hill and went into that little town like and just before I got to those buildings the French or the Germans had hay stacked it. They had stacked them up and all of a sudden about, I don't know how many of them just came apart with white flags hollering "comrade, comrade".

I was right in the middle of forty German soldiers by myself and I was scared to death. That's when my hair went straight up on my head, but they were hollering comrade, comrade; I need to tell you this, it's good.

The Germans put an SS troop with those polish soldiers. They didn't fight. The Germans also shot the polish soldiers so they had to fight, but anyway, I didn't know that there was an officer with them and I had the Polish, and they went over there and got on that German officer and was about to kill him, and I ran over there and got them off. I told them we need to interrogate him; I got to have him so we got them off.

I asked the German soldier, I could speak enough German and understood enough German that we could get by. I could do a little bit. I could get in trouble anyway. They wanted to give up so they surrendered so we started up the hill. I was in front of them; I wasn't behind them I was in front of them, and Sergeant Warder and the captain was looking in the binoculars saying , "my God, what has Joe Johnson done down there. What in the world."

Look there we got white flags coming, so he said they wasn't gonna fire cause Joe was with them. We got on up there and the captain said "Johnson, what you gonna do with these prisoners?" I said you the captain, that's your problem, not mine. He said "we ain't got no where to put these guys and one of them guys could speak a little English said "we want American uniforms and guns. We want to kill Germans."

We are Polish soldiers, we didn't want to fight to begin with, we want to fight for you, we want to join American Army, but George Patton wouldn't let them join, but they was honest and sincere about it.

You know, Hitler had captured all them countries over there. What we need to let the world know in history is Hitler had captured all those countries and took all the wealth and all the manpower down into Germany. His motive and his goal was to conquer the world, so the American soldiers had a world to save when we stormed that beachhead of Normandy. The world don't know that but they really need to read the history. It was a great honor to be in the service. I would do it again Brother Long in a minute.

JOHN LONG: All you fellows that I have talked to, you all knew you had a mission; you knew exactly what your mission was and what you needed to do.

JOE JOHNSON: Oh yeah, we knew exactly what our mission was.

JOHN LONG: Tell us about that time you went down there and smelled all those dead bodies.

JOE JOHNSON: Well, here again we were up into Germany; there was two big buildings down there, or three, I can't remember. I know there was two big ones. The Captain came down there and told Sergeant Warder to send a patrol down there and check those buildings out. I want to know what's in them buildings, and so here I am, I go down there again by myself and I opened the door on one of those buildings and I slammed it to cause it stunk so bad.

I said all those people are dead so they can't fire back at us. So I went back up there and said Sergeant Warder all them people in that building are dead. He said, "Joe, we got to have a head count, we will have to report how many people are dead in that building. I said Sergeant Warder, all them people in that building is dead, it smelled so bad, so Sergeant Warder said we got to go back down there.

He said come on Joe and go with me, so I went back down there with him and we opened the door, and Sergeant Warder said my heavens alive what in the world is that? When we got in there it was the Limburger Cheese Factory; so they called me cheese. My nickname was cheese the rest of my service.

JOHN LONG: We want this in there for sure. You got wounded with a piece of shrapnel in your leg and because you didn't go back to the back and stayed with your buddies you couldn't get a Purple Heart.

JOE JOHNSON: Well, when I got hit, I got hit with a German 88-mm. They was shelling us and that shell burst and that shrapnel hit me in the left leg. I was bleeding pretty good, and that shrapnel was hot and so I went back and Sergeant Warder had seen what had happened and I told him I had got hit. He looked at it and said you gonna have to go to the hospital. I said no, I am going down to the First Aid tent.

You need to know it was my fault I didn't get a Purple Heart, but I'll tell you why. If you left your organization you never got back with your organization. They sent you to somebody else. Whoever lost a man they will put you in that spot to fill it regardless of the organization. If you didn't have any training you were just a body, and we knew that and we had heard that. We had lost some people and they never got back to us, so I didn't want to. I asked the captain if I could just let the medics clean it every morning and dress it every morning and they did.

He said, "Joe, if it gets infected I got to send you to the hospital" and I agreed I would go to the hospital if it got infected, but those little medics were pretty good. They dressed it every morning and I was able to get that thing cleared up.

JOHN LONG: So you just got your medical treatment there?

JOE JOHNSON: At the CP camp, little medical camp

JOHN LONG: With the outfit rather than go back to the back where the hospital was?

JOE JOHNSON: Yeah, I didn't go to the hospital. They didn't make no record of it.

JOHN LONG: I can see when you are in that situation you feel so close to your buddies, your fellow soldiers that you don't want to leave them.

JOE JOHNSON: You are a band of brothers. When you train together you know what the people you train with can do. You know who you can depend on. That's very important in a war. You got to know who you are with. I didn't want to leave my organization; I wanted to stay with them.

JOHN LONG: As far as you are concerned, you don't have any bitterness because you didn't get the Purple Heart?

JOE JOHNSON: No, I don't have any bitterness.

JOHN LONG: You know what the rules were…

JOE JOHNSON: It was my fault. I wasn't trying to get glory and honor; I was trying to be a good solider. When I got discharged they asked me and I told them I was doing alright , and I wouldn't tell them because if I had they would have sent me to the hospital and that would have delayed me for weeks trying to run tests and getting all that information and I wanted to go home to the farm.

JOHN LONG: So you was ready to get out?

JOE JOHNSON: I was ready to get out.

JOHN LONG: You told me that you met your brother overseas in Paris? That's unusual…

JOE JOHNSON: Well, it's unusual. My Daddy wrote me a letter and said that my brother, Floyd, he was older than I was; he was in Dutch Harbor Alaska when the Japanese destroyed that up there. My brother was a combat engineer and Patton was needing combat engineers to put pontoons to get across those rivers so they called for them, so Floyd went to Paris but when he got there the war had ended by the time he got there.

My Daddy gave me his unit number and said that he was in Paris France, so I asked my captain if I could have a leave, and said yeah you got plenty of leave, where you going, and said I want to go R&R to Paris, so they gave me leave so I went down there.

I was looking his unit up and I was trying to figure out where his unit was and everything. I had everything I needed and I seen this guy coming down the street and he passed me and I said "Floyd Johnson, where are you going?" and he turned around and said "who the hell are you?" I said "I am Joseph." He said "what are you doing here?" I said same thing you are. He said how did you find out I was here, and I said Daddy wrote me a letter and told me you was down here in France. I ain't going to tell the whole story.

JOHN LONG: Nah, just enough to know it was unusual to know that he was actually up in the Pacific theater initially; I thought that was unusual.

JOE JOHNSON: It was unusual, it was a blessing.

JOHN LONG: Yeah, let's get back to the action you saw.

JOE JOHNSON: Oh yeah. After we crossed the Rhine River, we crossed another little river but I don't remember the name of that little ole river, but we crossed this river. It wasn't too wide but anyway we got on the other side and Sergeant Warder said to me Joe, get these binoculars and look around.

I said okay; but before we crossed that river I said, let me look and see what's over there, so I looked over there and the Germans were over there and had their shirts off, a German soldier had his shirt off and they had their pup tent. I told Sergeant Warder, I said Sergeant Warder, take these binoculars and look, they don't have their shirts on, look over there.

They are German, see them? I got up on a 40 mm gun placement and he said what you going to do, and I said I am going to turn this 40 mm around so I can fire at them. He said well lets just wait a minute. So I stood up on that gun placement and I heard this burp gun, the Germans shot a burp gun and there was green tracers going and I looked down between my legs and I seen green tracers coming through my legs.

That scared me to death. I jumped down in that gunner placement. Sergeant Wader said Joe, are you hit? I said I don't think I am and said but feel you and britches leg, them bullets were going through your britches leg, I can tell you that.

JOHN LONG: Was that the only time you got scared?

JOE JOHNSON: Lord, no, no, no, no, no. you know, Mr. Long, Harley Davidson has built a lot of motorcycles for Germany and they built a side car and those German officers they rode in a side car. A German soldier drove them around on that side car.

One day we knew they were coming towards us, we knew that. I heard this thing, it sounded different from a vehicle and I got to looking and I seen this side car. I said well look here. What in the world is that? I got on down there and we opened up fire and they got off of it and left.

They scattered when we started firing at them. I don't think we hit them, anyway we went up there and got the motorcycle and took the side car off and we decided we were going to ride that motorcycle.

We put that good American gas in there and boy that Harley Davidson would run good and that was a good motorcycle, and that was the first motorcycle I had seen that had a drive shaft. It didn't have a chain, it had a drive shaft.

We kept that thing about two or three weeks. We would take the ammo truck and move the ammo boxes over to the outside and put a rail in there and put something over it and then put the motorcycle up there and put stuff over it so the captain... we hauled it all over the place and one day he came down there and said Sergeant Warder, I got word that y'all got a motorcycle, who has got that motorcycle? If I catch ya'll with that motorcycle ya'll are in trouble.

JOHN LONG: What about the instances when you were in a fox hole? Tell us about being in a fox hole.

JOE JOHNSON: Well, here's the deal in a fox hole. Always when we pushed up and we sat down we always dug in because you never know who is going to throw a counter attack, you had to be ready. We would always dig in and would always sleep in a fox hole. What we would do, the Germans had these ole oak trees over there and we would cut; and had those gum trees like and Oak trees and we would cut some.

They would be about 4-5 inches around. We would cut them and we would dig a fox hole pretty deep then we would put that timber across there. We took that plastic stuff, that wax stuff that that powder come in and we laid that wax stuff down there. That was wax cardboard and we put dirt on that, about 8 inches of dirt over it, and if they had a shell burst that would protect you. We would sleep in those things at night.

JOHN LONG: Did they train you to dig a side hole to kick a hand grenade into? They trained us. You supposed to dig a pretty good size cave back in there so if a hand grenade comes in you try to get it up in that hole.

JOE JOHNSON: We didn't take that training, we took just digging with that little ole shovel we kept on our back in our backpacks. If you was scared you could dig like a ground mole.

JOHN LONG: What size hole did you wind up digging?

JOE JOHNSON: Big enough I could get this body into and turn crossways. If I couldn't get in there wide I would turn sideways.

JOHN LONG: Just depends I guess, on the dirt and how you could dig.

Joe Johnson at Battle of the Bulge

JOE JOHNSON: I need to tell you this. Up in the Ardennes Forest in Belgium near the battle of the bulge when we went up there we didn't know where we was going; we didn't know what we were going to do. We didn't have no earthly idea, but Patton had sent part of the

Third Army up there and we was gonna try to get those kids out of there.

We got up there; the Ardennes forest was the coldest place in the world. There ain't no deep freeze in the world as cold as that place was. It was so cold those kids were froze. They were lying on the ground. Some of them were still alive; you could pick them up and they were like fence posts. They couldn't bend their legs or nothing.

You just picked them up like fence posts just froze stiff. So many of those little kids froze to death, you just can't believe it. We had an old chow truck that had butane burners in it so we pulled the curtain down and started the stove up and put what we could in there; we had an ambulance, we sent some to the ambulance, but some many of those kids froze to death, it was a pitiful thing.

Lord that was pitiful, I need to tell you this. See, the Germans captured all of our equipment for the First Army. You know that, you know the history. Well, they captured all our trucks and all our tanks so this little guy from the south 40, he was a little farm boy, I don't know who he was, I never did find out his name, he told General Patton, he said well I can tell you how you can separate those tanks and the American Air Force can knock our own tanks out but there will be German people in it.

He said get you some florescence markings. Everyday you would have three stripes on there. He would put black, red, and orange on there today and tomorrow change that to green, blue and yellow, change it every morning and the Air Force will know what the code is and what the changes is and whoever don't change their codes they can knock those tanks out.

The Germans couldn't figure out why we were knocking them out with American tanks and they couldn't figure that out, so we destroyed all our own tanks and got rid of our

165

tanks and the Germans in them. They never did figure out what happened.

JOHN LONG: So ya'll colored the tanks?

JOE JOHNSON: Color coded the tanks. The Air Force could see it. You could see that florescence and they were down low enough when they started to fire at them they could tell. That little ole boy was pretty smart, he wasn't dumb.

JOHN LONG: We left this out early on, you got four Bronze Stars?

JOE JOHNSON: Yeah, four Bronze Stars.

JOHN LONG: And you was in Normandy battle and the battle of the budge and fierce fighting for Metz, and each one of those stars represents a battle?

JOE JOHNSON: Yeah, I wound up with four Bronze Stars.

Joe Johnson on American Women Heroes

JOE JOHNSON: So far so good, but I want to tell the American people what they really need to know; who the heroes were. The women in America, the United States women that lived in America in 1941 until 1945, went to the shipyards and the airplane factories and ammunition factories and built all our war machines and sent it to us.

They were the greatest generation of women this world will ever know. They were so great; let me tell you what those women done. If they had children most of the women had a brother, father or husband in war somewhere. They were in battle somewhere. The women stayed home. They were both mother and father and they took care of the home front.

Them women would take their children pawn them next door and go work eight hours in a defense factory and

166

when she came back in the evening after eight hours she would keep the ladies kids while she went and worked eight hours. This world don't know what a great blessing and sacrifice the American women sacrificed for World War II. They are the heroes. When we lost a tank they had three ready to go right up in the front. We never ran out of anything.

But I do need to tell you this story. It's kind of funny. After we crossed the Rhine River our ole driver hit something with the front wheel of the truck and busted a tire on it and they rolled the tire up there and was changing the tire and I sat down on the old tire while they were changing it, and I reached in my pack back there and got a K-ration. Them ole K-rations were terrible. Them crackers had been in there six months and they were stale. You could knock a dog in the head with them. In a K-ration you had little cans, they put three things in there; potted meat, corned beef hash and cheese.

JOHN LONG: What about the can opener about that size?

JOE JOHNSON: Yeah, oh yeah, I had one on my key. So one day we had been firing a lot and we threw everything in the fire and some of those cheese cans got thrown in there and when they swelled up and popped some of them hit my britches leg and I reached down trying to get it off of there and man we found out you could have a grilled sandwich with them cheeses, so everybody wanted cheese.

That black powder they shipped over there for those guns. That black powder they put in there for those shells. They packed the black powder in there; it came in a wax to keep water from damaging it before we get to it so we put all that wax stuff out there and burned it and it would burn like gas. We had to clean up everything. We didn't need to leave nothing.

JOHN LONG: What about the time you opened up your K-ration and it had a little note in there?

JOE JOHNSON: I was fixing to tell you, the boy hit something with the right front wheel and busted the tire. They were changing it and they rolled the old tire out there in the ditch.

I got a K-ration out of my pack back there. I went out there to sit down and eat, I was hungry, and opened the K-ration. When I opened it there was a little note in there. She said, "Soldier, I don't know who you are but my name is Shirley." I don't know if she said Davis or Ward, but it was one or the other, but her first name was Shirley.

She didn't give me her address or I would have wrote her. She said "I packed this especially for you, I hope you good luck and I hope you enjoy it. I packed this especially for you. I put two pieces of double mint chewing gum in there; I put you a bar of candy and three Chesapeake cigarettes. Extra!"

JOHN LONG: Now tell me more of your thought on the women of America.

JOE JOHNSON: Let me tell you, I had three sisters that worked in a defense factory and I had two sisters that worked for the Alabama Dry Dock Shipbuilding Company, and my older sister was a burner. She had an acetylene torch and she cut out those bulk heads for those tankers out on a ramp out there.

They had a ramp laid out there that had big poles out there and they laid those beams down on there and she had to cut those beams out. She had a helmet like a welding helmet and she had a jacket she wore, was a skin jacket, when that thing backfired; you know that ole burner it pops, you know what acetylene does, you have seen it pop. She would come home in the evenings and I would say, "Mary, my goodness, why don't you do something else" and she said "well, I am good at burning and I can do that, that's the best thing I can do. I like to cut steel out."

Mr. Long, its amazing what our American women done. The world needs to know that. You must remember, these women took care of their families, the home front, and still went to defense factories to ship all that stuff to us. There is no woman in the south, or in this country that didn't have a brother, husband or father in that war. They had one or the other in there. Some of them had all of them in there.

Joe Johnson sees Bob Hope and Doris Day

JOHN LONG: Tell me a pleasant memory.

JOE JOHNSON: When we were overseas Bob Hope came over there with Doris Day. You remember Doris Day?

JOHN LONG: Oh yeah.

JOE JOHNSON: Bob Hope brought Doris Day over there so we all went to the thing, and they told us to dig a latrine. We didn't have no bathroom, we dug a latrine; you know what a latrine is? And so Doris Day wanted to go to the bathroom, so she told Bob Hope, Bob, I got to go to the bathroom, where do I go? Bob said, well Doris, you don't got no bathroom here; you got to travel to that latrine down there. You know what, that crazy Bob Hope got up there and told that and we just died laughing. That Bob Hope was a card wasn't he?

JOHN LONG: Where were ya'll at when that was going on?

JOE JOHNSON: We were in Germany, I don't know what place, I don't remember, but we were in Germany. The USO came over there and entertained us.

JOHN LONG: Well, did she go down there and use the latrine?

JOE JOHNSON: Yeah, she had to. The boys hung pup tents on it with strings around there where you couldn't see her.

JOHN LONG: Doris Day was a good girl.

JOE JOHNSON: Oh yeah, we loved her. To see an American girl was exciting. She was a good performer, and that Bob Hope, he is crazy. He could laugh.

Joe Johnson with CIA "Clean-Up"

JOHN LONG: Is there anything else you can think we should cover?

JOE JOHNSON: It was such an honor to serve my country. I was so grateful for it. I was honored to serve this country, and I really felt I was a good soldier. I did my best. I did everything I could to do what I was supposed to do, and I was good. I could shoot down airplanes. I could knock them out of the sky. I was raised on a farm and I hunted squirrels and rabbits and I could knock their eyes out. I could take a 40mm, and I know I was good with it.

JOHN LONG: Have you got any more stories that you have thought of?

JOE JOHNSON: After the war was over if you landed on the Normandy Beach Head you got 86 points, so you see I had some high points. We had some guys in our unit that had wives and children and I wasn't married so I gave them my slot to come back to the states and I would take theirs and stay over there.

I kept giving back, and the captain told me one day, Joe, I don't want you to do that, I want you to go home. I said well look, they got children and they need to go home; I am not married and I am doing alright. He said, well I tell you what we gonna do, we are going to assign you to work with the CIA, the Central Intelligence Agency.

So I said okay. I was assigned to work with Carl Smith, he was a full Colonel; an Eagle Colonel.

I drove for Colonel Smith and one day he told me, said Joe, there is a new jeep down there, go down there and get it and take it to the motor pool. They know what to do with it. I said okay, so I took it down there and I told that Sergeant Colonel Smith said for me to bring this jeep down here and you would know what to do with it, and he said "I don't know what to do with it," and I said well you better call him he told you what to do with it and when I went back down there to get it about five o'clock that evening they had took the backseats out of the jeep and welded a big ole post in the back and they put rings on that post.

JOHN LONG: Did they weld the rings to the posts?

JOE JOHNSON: Yeah, the rings were welded to the posts; and so I didn't know what was going on so when I got the jeep I told Colonel Smith they ruined my jeep. He said, no I tell you what we gonna do, so the first thing he said was tomorrow morning we going to Innsbruck Austria; that's the most beautiful place in Germany. There ain't no prettier place in Germany as Innsbruck Austria.

I said what are we going up there for and he said I'll tell you what we are gonna do, so we went up there. The other agents had picked up this SS trooper, you know, that had gassed the Jews.

They was those bad people. They were mean. So, we went to get him. The Colonel told me Joe, open that box and get those handcuffs out of there. Then I began to realize what them rings on those posts were for.

When the CIA agents brought this guy out there they said, Colonel Smith and Private Johnson, I'll tell you something right now, this guy is going to get away just as sure as you

171

are sitting here. He is the meanest guy we have picked up
and he is going to kill both of you if he can.

I said he ain't going to kill me, so I put handcuffs on him
and then handcuffed him to that steel post in that jeep, then
I put another one on him and then I put one on his foot, and
you know what? I said I bet you don't go no where.

He told me that he was an exchange student that went to
Chicago and Detroit. He learned a little English and he
said to me, driver what happens if you turn this jeep over
and I said throw me and colonel out, you on the bottom and
he said that ain't fair, and I said well you started this war.

We went all over Europe picking up those SS troopers,
those guys that did all that killing.

JOHN LONG: Also, you told me that you actually
personally blew up one of those crematoriums. We'll
discuss that a bit later. It wasn't long after that that you
came back to the states?

Joe Johnson After the War

JOE JOHNSON: It wasn't all that long. One day I was
gone with Colonel Smith somewhere, we had a telegram.
The Red Cross had sent a telegram and the colonel got it.
He said Joe; you got a telegram for something. My Daddy
had sent to the Red Cross, look my son was on Normandy
Beach Head and he needs to come home.

I want him home, so they said you got thirty minutes. They
got a boat leaving out of Bremerhaven Germany going
back to New York. You got thirty minutes to get your stuff
ready. They carried me in a jeep down there. Everybody
else had done loaded on it. It was a converted cattle ship.
It took us seventeen days to come back across the Atlantic.

JOHN LONG: They only gave you thirty minutes notice
before they put you on a ship?

JOE JOHNSON: Yeah, I packed some and left some. You know how the military is. When they get in a hurry march order means march order. I got my duffle bag and run.

JOHN LONG: So did you come back to New York?

JOE JOHNSON: Yeah, came by the Statute of Liberty, and you know what? That was a great feeling to see the Statute of Liberty. That was a blessing.

JOHN LONG: Did you get seasick coming back?

JOE JOHNSON: Whew, yes I did. I wouldn't be a sailor. You couldn't hire me to be a sailor. I really got sick coming back and in that English Channel. That English Channel is rough water itself.

JOHN LONG: What kind of work did you do when you got back?

JOE JOHNSON: Well, after the war was over, after I got home and got a discharge I came home I met my wife; it wasn't very long, about three or four weeks and we got married and I have been with her 67 years so she's a jewel. I found a good one.

I went to work at Brookley Air Force Base in Mobile Alabama.

One day my boss told me he had an assignment for me.

Said he was going to send me TDY. I said where we going and he said it's secret and we can't tell you, we can't tell you what it is. He said you need to get six men and an operator, including yourself. He said I will tell you where you going, we will give you the orders, we can't tell you, but when you leave here we will give you the orders and it will tell you where to go.

So I guess it was a couple of days I give him all the names. He had to get them cleared and get them cleared for secret. I told him I wanted W.C. Strayhand out of Lucedale, MS, and he said why you want him. I said ole W.C. can operate a piece of equipment more than anybody I have ever seen. He is good.

He said Joe, here's your orders. He gave it to us in an envelope, in a brown envelope. It was just regular size. It said "confidential, secret". He said now Joe you can't open this envelope until you get to Citronelle Alabama, forty or fifty miles out of Mobile.

When I opened the envelope it said report to the base at Huntsville Alabama.

We were escorted to a big round table and the officer said you have been sent here to train on a Jupiter missile. We gonna put a satellite on the nose of that missile that you going to move to Vandenberg CA to put the first satellite around the world. I said Carl, what is a satellite? Here I am moving a satellite and I have never heard of it. We trained on a Jupiter missile for 21 days, off and on, Jupiter missile. It weighed 45,000 pounds and was 45 foot long.

I worked on various programs until I retired in 1985 and went back to the farm.

JOHN LONG: Well, I think we have pretty well covered it. If we have left out something you can...

JOE JOHNSON: I think we pretty well covered everything.

JOHN LONG: It's been such a pleasure talking with you Mr. Johnson.

JOE JOHNSON: It's a blessing.

"Rabbit" Kennedy D-Day Experiences

When D-Day came my outfit did not go on the first wave. We had to trade those 2-1/2 ton trucks in for a big heavy weight artillery self-propelled artillery and they had to wait until the infantry cleared the beaches so we could go ashore in them heavy artillery pieces.

It was six days after D-Day when we landed in Normandy.

I search my mind and my memory. Everybody had D-Day on their mind, because they knew if you were in the infantry that you were going to hit the beaches horrible. Like me, I was in this heavy duty tank type artillery. I knew I had some protection from small arms fire, but it was horrible to see what happened.

JOHN LONG: When you got to Omaha Beach you described the horrible aspect of it, and this was six days after D-Day. Did you observe anything a little more specific about your observations; let's say about the landing craft that was still in the water and some of the gunning placements that may have been up on the higher ground up on Omaha Beach.

RABBIT KENNEDY: Well, the Germans occupied the high ground really because they had the Americans down below them. They were on the coast and the Americans in the LSTs, landing crafts, and the Germans just had an open field of fire to kill all the Americans and later on I read about the weather.

The bodies were still floating out in the water that Germany had sank the LSTs, dead soldiers everywhere. The only thing that kept them floating was the heavy packs they had on them, used really to help the guy to stay without drowning, but the Germans kept shooting and killing everybody them packs just kept the bodies from going down and whatever....

The weather was rough, turned bad the night that the D-Day invasion was taking place the next morning and them LSTs were capsizing and when the Germans were firing and knocking a hole in one it would sink right away and then the Americans would be out trying to get ashore, wading ashore and the Germans would just kill them. They didn't have no protection.

And from that day on we walked, we marched, across France and the fighting in the hedgerows was hard.

"Rabbit" Kennedy Beyond the Beach

Them Germans would dig in them hedgerows and camouflage themselves good and when the infantry came up close to them they would kill everyone.

We walked all across France. As a young soldier I will never forget. When we got into Germany the Germans had them big 88 long tom artillery pieces and Tiger tanks. The Americans didn't have nothing to penetrate those tanks with.

"Rabbit" Kennedy re Battle of Bulge

On Thanksgiving Day, 1943, I guess, the Germans attacked it and that's when they killed all the Americans in sleeping bags. The weather was bad, heavy snow, heavy fog, the planes couldn't bomb them because they couldn't see.

Infantry lost so many people, for instance 102nd Infantry Division we were supporting for artillery fire, but they lost so many infantry and couldn't get replacements that they took a lot of guys like me, artillery type, tank type guys and made infantry out of them. We fought there for seems like forever and every day they would haul out dead people, frozen in their foxholes. I became a grown man overnight. I said that if the good Lord will just bless me and let me get home I would always remember to be good to people, because the good Lord was taking care of us.

JOHN LONG: There was one mention; I guess it was at the Battle of the Bulge, where you had to be in a foxhole with a dead German soldier.

RABBIT KENNEDY: That was at Hurtgen Forest. That was the 102nd Infantry Division in there protecting the tanks, you know the artillery pieces, and when the German column came down the road and all the infantry, the German Infantry men was riding on the German tank, the Tiger 88, I will never forget it, and they would get off and kill the American infantry men.

So the guy that was in the foxhole with me, I was in B Battery and he was in A Battery, same outfit, he got gut shot, you know guts hanging out, but we didn't have no medical evacuation and whatever. They had to depend on the medical people assigned, the aid men they called them, the medical aid men.

Some of them got killed right away so the guy didn't have a chance. It was cold and snowing. I will never forget when that guy died he was coughing and I knew he was dying then. He was bleeding inside. I remember that whenever they passed, a guy in a jeep would come throw out C-rations by each foxhole. He wouldn't stop he would just throw it out and keep on going because he would get shot by the Germans.

I never did know the guy, except that he was from A Battery. I was from B Battery. I would see him around, but I never knew what his name was.

JOHN LONG: What about some of your friends that you made back then, in other words, that was in your outfit that you got to be buddies with and so forth. Do you recall any of the friendships and what happened to some of your friends and all that?

RABBIT KENNEDY: That's right. One guy up on the Ebb River, that's where we met the Russians, and the mesh truck got hit, a direct hit, and there was a guy, he survived.

He lives in Tupelo, Mississippi now. His name is James Wesley Rollan. He was a cook, and he was from Baldwyn, Mississippi when he went in the Army. I never knew what happened to him until after the war was over. He got hit and I never did know how bad it was, but he survived. I don't know whether he is still living or not. I don't know.

Other than that, my experience in Germany during that period was horrible, cold, cold weather. I felt so sorry for the French. The French were eating out of the garbage can where the Americans would go through the chow line and dump what they didn't eat in big ole garbage cans, the women and the children of the French would gather up every morning and get that garbage out and put it in a pan and walk across the fields of snow and cold weather going home, but they had something to eat.

JOHN LONG: Did you ever encounter any German prisoners that you spoke with or anything like that?

RABBIT KENNEDY: The Germans were taking American prisoners and marching them down the road and the Americans were trying to kill the Germans, but I am satisfied in my mind that a lot of Americans got killed by the fire between the Americans and the Germans.

JOHN LONG: I had one gentleman tell me that one German they captured asked him why are you a day late, because the weather had postponed it from June the 5th

178

until June the 6th, so that told the fellow that I talked to that the Germans knew exactly what day they were supposed to come across but they didn't come that day they came the next day. Did you...

RABBIT KENNEDY: I was just a private, I didn't know the big picture, but when Eisenhower got briefed by the weather people they told him the weather was going to be bad but he didn't change the date. He says that we prepared to go on the 6th so we are going on the 6th. The Germans knew everything we were doing. I am sure they had spies in the French country and they was reporting everything they saw.

JOHN LONG: Some of the fellows talked about that they had been placed, before the invasion, they put them in like stockades, they pinned them in with Constantine wire and everything and they couldn't get out to just before the invasion. Did you have that same experience?

RABBIT KENNEDY: I didn't know that. Only thing I knew was the Americans would take care of American prisoners and whenever the bombers or the fighter planes would start scraping the Germans, the Germans would make the Americans stay in the road hoping the planes wouldn't scrape no more on account of Americans there and prisoners of war.

But the only thing I remember, I can't remember the name of the towns or the river, but the river, the Americans was all hunkered down on the banks of the river, the bombers had knocked out the bridges so the Germans couldn't keep coming into France.

I remember they would be hunkered down. I saw a lot of American soldiers killed. I don't know who killed them, but regardless of who killed them a lot of our soldiers didn't come home.

JOHN LONG: Back to the French aspect of it. You talked about the French women and children eating out of the garbage cans and so forth, tell us a little bit more of your experiences involving the Normandy area and where this was taking place.

RABBIT KENNEDY: In Normandy, I believe, if I am correct, they had three landing sites. One was a decoy so the Germans would think that is where the main body was going on at, but that wasn't just where the main body was. Normandy is where the main body hit and there was just a low area but it had high bluffs on the edge of the water...

JOHN LONG: Yeah, Normandy was the only real invasion site.

RABBIT KENNEDY: Yeah. See, I don't know, I heard that the people, the Germans were being fed by the French. They were scared of them and the French were feeding them. Whether that is so or not I don't know because the French was trying to survive themselves; eating out of the garbage cans and things like that.

I guess if De Gaulle hadn't been a friend of the Americans we wouldn't have survived France. The French formed their own freedom fighters and they joined the Americans. I got to see them. They had an American uniform on and a French flag sewed on their shoulder patch. That's the difference we could tell that they was French.

I don't know sir, the French has been our allies, I guess, for centuries, but they did have a lot of traitors and you could see a guy hanging. We would go down the road, you know, marching the column down the road and pass a farmhouse and you could see; I know in two cases where two farmers had been hung by their neighbors. They had become traitors to the French and the neighbors had hung them.

JOHN LONG: The French farmers that got hung were aiding and abetting the Germans?

RABBIT KENNEDY: That's right.

JOHN LONG: Then after the Americans landed and kind of took control they took care of the traitors?

RABBIT KENNEDY: That's right. They would go back and become heroes you might say, but in essence they was a traitor to the French Government.

JOHN LONG: That's interesting. What's your best recollection of what town you remember up there near Normandy that you went into?

RABBIT KENNEDY: Oh, I used to see a sign everywhere we would turn that would say St. Lo...St. Lo France. Every road led, not to Paris, but I would see St. Lo, and that's where the heavy fighting was going on also. When they moved the troops from the southern invasion of France and Patton's unit invaded St. Lo with all the tanks. It was tank country down there, but I always wondered how big St. Lo was because every sign I saw with an arrow pointing towards St. Lo.

JOHN LONG: Is there anything else that you want to throw in here about the Normandy invasion aspect you can think of?

RABBIT KENNEDY: Only thing I can remember was the Red Cross had people, as strange as it may seem, them women that run the, Donut Dolly, as they called it, I don't know where they got the donuts, but they would come along in a jeep with a red cross on it and hand out what they could and they was real, real great Americans. A lot of soldiers got a donut and a cup of coffee.

JOHN LONG: Without going into a whole lot of detail about the Battle of the Bulge, tell us from the time the war ended what you did.

Rabbit Kennedy After the War

RABBIT KENNEDY: When the war was over guys like me that volunteered had the opportunity to be the first ones discharged and sent home, but I didn't want to, I wanted to keep fighting the Jap's. At a place called Camp Lucky Strike, they were processing people to go to Japan, and I volunteered there, and on the way round through the Panama Canal and up the west coast of California take on resupplies or whatever the war was over.

The atomic bomb had been dropped, and I was so proud of that.

JOHN LONG: Tell me more about Camp Lucky Strike.

RABBIT KENNEDY: Camp Lucky Strike? That was a salvation when you heard them talking about Camp Lucky Strike, you knew you were going home, hopefully. You had to have certain points. I will never forget, the points was 90, and I had 93 points because I had prior service and I had volunteered and the First Sergeant, when the war was over, and the people that didn't have the points were assigned to Army of Occupation, and all the other guys, like myself, unless you volunteered were going home, but I volunteered and a lot of others did, to fight the Jap's.

They would send us to the Captain and issue us all new uniforms and whatever and sent you home for thirty days. Then when you got home you reported back and they put you on a train at Camp Kilmer New Jersey. That's where they put me on a train and sent me to Camp Shelby for a thirty day furlough.

I got to Camp Shelby and they processed me as a volunteer going to Japan. They sent me to Amory, Mississippi. We hired a cab; three of us did, from Camp Shelby to come to Amory, Mississippi. One guy lived at Amory beside me, and I think the other one lived in Tupelo.

We hired a cab to come from Camp Shelby. It charged us $30 to come home, and then we had to report back on our own. When we got back they sent us down to a place in Alabama; it was a prisoner of war camp down there, Ellisville Alabama, and they loaded us on buses and sent us down to Florida and we got on a boat. We went through the Panama Canal, up the coast of California and Mexico to take on the way to...

JOHN LONG: Somewhere in the Pacific probably...

RABBIT KENNEDY: I believe we were on our way to Hawaii, I believe. The war was over and I was glad of that.

JOHN LONG: How did you get back home after that?

RABBIT KENNEDY: To get back home, they dropped us off at Crooksville, on the California coast at Camp Cook California, and we stayed there. I though we never would get a break. It was always cold and wind blowing. We finally left there and they sent us to Camp Chaffee Arkansas and from there they discharged me and sent me on.

JOHN LONG: So you were discharged in Chaffee Arkansas.

RABBIT KENNEDY: Yeah.

JOHN LONG: And then you came on home. [Since we are talking to Rabbit Kennedy, he made a career out of the military and was in there for 35 years, past Normandy and the Battle of the Bulge and the European theater.] So you ever have a period of time when you wasn't in the military?

RABBIT KENNEDY: Yes. Yes I did. After I came home I thought, I had $800 I had saved up. I thought that would be enough money to last me forever. I never saw $800, and now I spent my money as a young soldier and I went broke so I had to go back in the Army.

JOHN LONG: So you went back in there and wound up with a short tour in Korea and a pretty long tour in Vietnam.

RABBIT KENNEDY: Two long tours in Vietnam, hard. Vietnam was the worse war I ever attended. It was worse than World War II. All the things that happened to the soldiers in World War II, Vietnam was worse.

Living conditions in Vietnam for the 1st Calvary Division, and I was Sergeant Major of an infantry battalion. I was a division Sergeant Major and the American soldiers in Vietnam could not get shoes to wear. They would rot off their feet.

That's right. I have seen soldiers make sandals out of rubber, old tires, because it was monsoon season, it would rain all the time, shoes would rot and the soldiers; it wasn't cold. That's the only thing that saved us, it wasn't cold over there.

JOHN LONG: I believe you retired from the military in '75?

RABBIT KENNEDY: '75, sir.

JOHN LONG: So that meant that you was in there right at 35 years?

RABBIT KENNEDY: Yes, sir.

JOHN LONG: Since you retired in 1975 kind of tell us how you readjusted to civilian life.

RABBIT KENNEDY: I just adjusted. Well, I tell you how I adjusted, I married, had a good wife. We had two children. I had advanced to the rank of Command Sergeant Major and I just loved it and I always had a saying when I was in the Army as a Command Sergeant Major, I could move hundreds of people with a telephone call but when I retired I couldn't get a little dirt hauled; but that's alright.

I could cope with that. I got a job, retired, love my country and love the people and thank the good Lord that I never did get a scratch.

JOHN LONG: This is a pretty tough question because it goes like this: How your war time experiences affected your life? In other words, I guess looking back now after all these years what perspective do you think that your war time experiences, especially in the first one, in Normandy, the one we are concerned with.

RABBIT KENNEDY: Well, as a young guy, and Normandy, as a young guy doing a career and whenever I experienced that two years in Vietnam under horrible conditions, I was a family man trying to survive, take care of my family and I didn't think it was going to affect me. I thought I was too tough for that and that wasn't the case.

Ten years after retirement I lost my mind. I lost my mind temporarily.

JOHN LONG: Was that kind of like post-traumatic stress?

RABBIT KENNEDY: Yeah. I am speaking for myself and not for all them. About 70% of the soldiers that went to Vietnam, they documented it; about 70% came back an alcoholic, dope addict, or divorced. World War II you never heard of that. The guys would go over there, fight for his country, come home and rejoin his family and got a job and went on but Vietnam was different.

JOHN LONG: I have got a question that has been in my mind since I was lucky enough to never have to serve in combat, but to me war is a useless, worthless thing in most instances, however, in World War II it was a different cause that everybody had and a lot of fellows have asked the question, even in that war and other wars, why am I here. I think you have made that statement before when we chatted.

RABBIT KENNEDY: Why am I here? I am going to give you a good example. In Vietnam, going back to Vietnam now, I am an older man, I am forty something years old, I am a Command Sergeant Major and had a lot of responsibilities and I made this statement time and time again:

Me and my commanding General would go to visit hospitals on Sundays; you know we would stay in the jungles and the Command General and me would go from one battle area to another in a helicopter, and on Sunday we went to a hospital in Saigon where the troops had got ambushed in the 1st or 7th Calvary and lost a lot of people, they done lost two companies in one battalion.

In the hospital there were two guys there, one guys legs was blowed off and the other guy was shot up in the stomach and the chest and the general was talking to them; General Turner talked a lot at us and I wouldn't talk to them two guys, and one guy said, and I will never forget it, Sergeant Major call my wife.

We could use telephone conversations in Vietnam that we didn't have in World War II and I used the General's authority to call on the phone to tell his wife that he loved her and he is crying. I knew I was choking up, so I walked outside.

When the General and me walked outside I couldn't hold it no longer, I broke down, saying how useless we was in Vietnam, saying to myself why are we here. You got me. I supported our Commander in Chief, I was supporting our country, but at the same token I had a lot of questions in my mind, are we really doing the right thing, and so I cried, and the general, he was a two star general, he saw me crying and he came and put his arm around my shoulder and he said Sergeant Major, go ahead and cry.

I said to him, and it became world-wide, comment that was made throughout the world, a comment by me, I said "I must be weak, I can't stop from crying" and the general said to me, Sergeant Major, cry all you want to, I wouldn't let my daughter marry a man that wouldn't cry. I never forgot that. At the same token I always ask myself, why are we here, why, why, why, why. God bless you.

Olin McKee D-Day Experiences

JOHN LONG: Tell us what you remember of D-Day. I know it was 20 days after D-Day when you went to the Normandy beaches.

OLIN MCKEE: Yeah, we got the news American and British forces had landed on the coast of France. That was D-Day. It was only after a matter of days before they needed the big stuff to break the defense walls.

Our battalion had started in late May to start marshalling our equipment. We loaded our equipment onto LSTs and liberty ships which made a bridge of both from the English ports to Omaha Beach.

JOHN LONG: My goodness, I never realized they had them lined all the way across the channel.

OLIN MCKEE: Oh yeah.

JOHN LONG: What your best recollection on what you did first after you got the artillery pieces onto the shore and went inland with them?

OLIN MCKEE: I don't recall anything outstanding at all. Of course everybody was frightened at that time. We were all just kids going to war.

187

JOHN LONG: Were you under fire when you landed?

OLIN MCKEE: No.

JOHN LONG: Did you ever get under fire?

OLIN MCKEE: Oh yes.

JOHN LONG: Do you have any recollection about where you were in Normandy at the time you were under fire?

OLIN MCKEE: No. I can see it, but I can't tell you, I can't call the name to it or anything.

JOHN LONG: Okay, just tell me what you visualized.

OLIN MCKEE: We were very fortunate. My company didn't lose but one man during the entire war, and we usually fought if the Germans were getting the best of us so to speak, that's when we would come into place, and we could shoot over our infantry.

JOHN LONG: Did you actually have to go forward and be a forward observer some?

OLIN MCKEE: We had some, but I did not, but we had some.

JOHN LONG: What about the hedgerows, getting through them and so forth. Did they already have them kind of peeled away? Was there any problem getting through the hedgerows?

OLIN MCKEE: We done pretty good. We were, one day, I was with the captain and each company was going out to find a suitable fire place. You couldn't just put those guns up anywhere. You had to have a place to get into it. That particular time we had a driver and the captain, the radio operator and myself.

We located an area that we thought would be a good area for our gun and the captain told me to stay there with the driver and the radio operator and he went on with another company to help them find a location.

I was kind of nosy. We were parked, our vehicle was parked on a high embankment, probably 15 foot high embankment and the infantry had had a pretty good battle in that area. That was obvious. There was a pasture over here and a pretty good patch of woods and I was sitting there in the car just waiting on time and decided to get out and I got out and climbed up that embankment, road embankment, and looking down in the woods there was a body that had on American camouflage.

I assumed it was an American. I started to go down, when I first saw it, I started to go down and see if I could be of any help, I kept watching and all of a sudden he blinked and so I got back to the car and called the captain and they came back there. It ended up we got three Germans out of that patch of woods that had been in combat the day before.

The Germans that were not hurt; they were just left behind or something. We got them started back to the compound and one of them reached in his pocket and pulled out a hand grenade. He had been searched by four or five people.

How he hid that grenade we will never know. He pulled it out and threw it out but didn't pull the trigger on it, just threw it away because he got too close and he knew if he went into the American compound with that he would get killed.

That was one of the biggest scares I had when I saw this fellow, thinking it was a dead American and it turned out to be a live German. I didn't see but one at that time, but when we went back and got them out of there; there were three of them.

JOHN LONG: None of those guys were wounded?

189

OLIN MCKEE: No. They were waiting to give themselves up or either got lost from their outfit. It was obvious there had been a pretty good fight the day before that.

JOHN LONG: Any other things that you can recall similar to that, like the Germans playing possum? What about some funny things. It's natural to suppress the bad memories but the good memories you normally retain.

OLIN MCKEE: I was supposed to be going back to get some ammunition. I filled in several different responsibilities, and at that time really my responsibility was ammunition. I forget whether there was two or three trucks I was taking to get more ammunition, and I was of course in the lead truck, and come into kind of houses. There was two if I remember right good looking German girls out there in the field.

JOHN LONG: Were these German girls or French?

OLIN MCKEE: French. Anyway, they threw up their hand and we threw up ours; flirting and carrying on. We went on and got the ammunition. I forget whether it was three or four, but anyway there were several trucks.

We got loaded and when we come back, it was late in the afternoon, so that give me a good excuse, so we were going to pull over in this field. It was about as far as from me to her to where these girls were that we assumed lived. To turn off of the main road I had one of the trucks come in and it was too far to the left and flipped the truck. I just knew I was going to the brig over that.

We ended up having to stay that night with the trucks and the next morning we took the other two or three trucks, I forgot just exactly how many, on in with what ammunition we had and reported up there to the captain. I was a Buck Sergeant and pulled it up there to the captain and told him what had happened, and I can't tell you what he said. He ended up saying "Sergeant, can't you do nothing right?" He told me just go on back and get the truck, and I had to go back and winch that truck over and bring it on in.

We had been without hot food or anything for so long and down in one of the valleys these two beautiful girls were down there milking the cows and we got so excited that we had not had milk for so long that we actually went down and drank milk straight from the cows.

JOHN LONG: They squirted it directly from the cow into your mouths?

JOHN LONG: Tell us about the bridge at Remagen that the Germans tried to blow up and they couldn't blow it up and that's the only one left across the Rhine.

OLIN MCKEE: Yeah, I was there.

JOHN LONG: Since you started off as a PFC and the Captain said "can't you do anything right" how in the world did you get to be a First Sergeant?

OLIN MCKEE: I don't know. I always tried to do my job. This fellow, Captain Reese was one. He was our captain. Someway he took a liking to me. I think he and his wife had three or four kids and had adopted three or four, and I think he took me on as a kid.

JOHN LONG: Since you was the youngest kid in the outfit.

OLIN MCKEE: I think so.

JOHN LONG: You was the only kid in the outfit as far as he was concerned, I see.

OLIN MCKEE: Of course on those big guns it took a lot of hard work; protecting the guns and setting them up.

JOHN LONG: If I understand it right, Paris caved in when the Germans invaded France and they didn't get the destruction. There wasn't any war there, they just capitulated, that Paris and Versi was pretty well intact.

[Affirmative nod.]

JOHN LONG: So you were involved in probably the first artillery pieces to fall on German soil?

OLIN MCKEE: I think that's right.

JOHN LONG: Sounds right. If it wasn't the first it was right there early on, wasn't it?

OLIN MCKEE: It was right there.

JOHN LONG: Do you recall this happy time, going through Paris.

OLIN MCKEE: We had a good time.

JOHN LONG: It wouldn't be hard to have any time would be a good time under those circumstances.

OLIN MCKEE: For some reason, I don't know why, I was the youngest in the outfit, as far as I know. I didn't have any responsibility. We had Babcock, was one of the buddies that would have a problem at home. Most of them were married in my outfit. They were married men. I was the smallest in age wise.

Olin McKee at Battle of the Bulge

JOHN LONG: Your sister said that there was a time when you said, we almost lost the war.

OLIN MCKEE: Yeah, we were on the verge of that. I don't remember all the details, but we took too much for granted, and during one period of time we thought there for a little bit we were going to lose out, but of course we built back up and went on and done our job. It was pretty touchy there for a while.

192

JOHN LONG: That sounds like it was more, at that point in time, was more like where the Battle of the Bulge occurred.

OLIN MCKEE: Yeah, that is what we are talking about. The bulge became a pocket and the Germans lost more than 100,000 men and much equipment. The Ardennes Forest interlude was finished.

JOHN LONG: Now, you said a while ago that you only lost one man in your outfit. Did that come from enemy fire?

OLIN MCKEE: Yes.

JOHN LONG: Do you recall when or where, or something about that particular battle? They had to shoot a pretty good ways since ya'll have a 14 mile range.

OLIN MCKEE: I can see it in the face, but I don't know how to tell you where it was. I have forgotten what the area was. It was towards the end of the war, and we had captured two Germans that they were not supposed to be there. They were in the same area we were in, and it ended up that one of them we had to shoot. We of course tried to fix him up, but I can't remember what that area was but it was towards the end of the war.

JOHN LONG: These Germans, ya'll thought you had already cleared this out and they were just kind of hanging back.

OLIN MCKEE: Right.

Olin McKee After the War

JOHN LONG: Okay, what about back with your family. Coming home, did they meet you at the train or did you just kind of slip in on them or what?

OLIN MCKEE: No, I didn't slip in. She can tell you more about that than I can.

[His sister describes a great home coming.]

JOHN LONG: I can see he is still a little emotional about that…. What about readjustment, the period of trying to lay it aside what you had been through and trying to get back to doing what you did the rest of your civilian life?

OLIN MCKEE: I done the best I could to just get rid of all of it in my mind.

JOHN LONG: Did you ever have this problem that they have nowadays and talk about all the time, like nightmares or flashbacks?

OLIN MCKEE: I have had dreams. I don't remember having any real dangerous to myself, but I have had some dreams of parts of the war.

I think it made a better man out of me, more responsibility, and I think it was a benefit, just like Christine was talking about, I think that helped me to be a better man. I have worked basically ever since I came back. I was working with Lance Packing Company, of course I got tired of that and took some courses, GI courses in engineering and that type of thing. I think it made a better man out of me.

[Sister: He has never failed to fly the flag; you probably saw the American flag. The flag has been a part of his life, as in all of ours, but particularly him. He is proud of our flag.]

JOHN LONG: Oh yeah. It wouldn't be here if we hadn't…

OLIN MCKEE: That's right. It made a better man out of me.

JOHN LONG: Is there anything that we have not covered that needs to be said?

OLIN MCKEE: I don't know of anything in particular. I will agree with the man that said "war is hell," but it made a better man out of me. It made me grow up more so.

JOHN LONG: The whole idea is that somewhere down the road it will be second-hand accounts. It won't be any more first-hand accounts.

[Affirmative nod.]

JOHN LONG: I want to tell you it has been a great pleasure meeting with you here sir.

OLIN MCKEE: I appreciate it.

George Pulakos Experiences on D-Day

JOHN LONG: What beach did you land on?

GEORGE PULAKOS: Omaha Beach.

JOHN LONG: You went straight to Omaha. Were you there along at Pointe du Hoc?

GEORGE PULAKOS: I didn't know where we were. As far as being oriented all the time I was in the battle it was hard for me to orient. I would swear that we were going this direction and being shot at and the next day we were reversing and was still being shot at. I was never really good at it. I can remember landing. I could look over to my left and see the cliffs that the rangers were trying to climb the cliff.

JOHN LONG: When you landed you could see them trying to climb?

195

GEORGE PULAKOS: I could see them way in the distance. We, of course, when you first land you head for something that is in front of you and bury your nose.

JOHN LONG: Head for cover in other words.

GEORGE PULAKOS: It was the most frightening experience I have ever had. Then, we almost got pushed back and almost got thrown off the beach and the Navy saved us. Somebody gave the order to use the Navy guns. They turned the tide for us.

JOHN LONG: When you, did you go in an LCT.

GEORGE PULAKOS: Coming off, yeah. We came across the channel we were put on a ship. It landed, it stopped quite a ways. They had sunk a lot of ships in the water because there was a bit of a storm, and we climbed down a rope and got into these landing crafts and we would head for the beach.

JOHN LONG: One fellow said that he saw some of the landing crafts get overloaded and sink.

GEORGE PULAKOS: Well, what happened to us is we were on the United States landing craft run by the Coast Guard. We were going over and the line got hung up on a sunken ship. The medics were loaded in the back of the landing craft so the troops would go out first and we would follow and pick up the wounded so to speak.

We got hung up on this ship and a British landing craft came and went nose to nose and we reloaded onto that. Now, instead of being at the back of it I was in the front. I remember one fellow with me that was also in the medic unit, named James Long, he was 6 foot 2 or 3.

The landing craft came to a crunch and dropped the front end of it down, he stepped off and he went into water up to his nose. He had all this equipment, medical packs. I knew if I stepped off it was going to be well over my head, so I grabbed the chain and swung around and scampered to the back of it. I wasn't going to step off. When a few of them got off...

JOHN LONG: A while ago you said that you initially had troops in the front and medics in the rear. What proportion of troops to medics did they put in the landing craft?

GEORGE PULAKOS: At the time we went in we had a large landing craft and only six medics at the back and the rest troops. They were in no particular outfit. Some were tank drivers. There was a mixture of personnel going in there.

JOHN LONG: That sounds kind of disorganized doesn't it?

GEORGE PULAKOS: Well, I didn't find out until years later that actually they were to have tank support on the beach, but the tanks, because it was storming, I guess the guys that drove tanks weren't sailors. All of those tanks got sunk in the landing. We were to replace any medics that got killed and they were going to replace any tank drivers that got killed, but the tanks never got there.

JOHN LONG: The most interesting, and probably one of the most famous aspects was the rangers climbing the cliffs. Can you elaborate about that?

GEORGE PULAKOS: It was way down in the distance. I could just see. Billy and I remember it; thank God I am not a ranger.

JOHN LONG: Did you ever know why they had to take the cliffs?

GEORGE PULAKOS: No idea, I just saw them. Then, finally we got a foothold and they pushed them back away from the edge and I still was on the beach. They kept me on the beach. I could swim. I was a swimmer, and I would recover bodies. I would go out in the water and recover bodies. We were stacking them like cord wood on the beach.

JOHN LONG: About how long did that go on?

GEORGE PULAKOS: I was on that beach, after they pushed them back a little, it must have been a week that we stayed on the beach, and then the 83rd Division came in and they were to go up and relieve the paratroopers that had jumped in behind the lines. They came in and they assigned me…well they didn't assign me at first.

The 83rd Division went in and they tried to cross a sea swamp, marsh and sea water, and the Germans knocked off about 60 percent of them by shooting the flack guns up into the trees and when they came back I replaced the medic on the 83rd Division. That was probably near the end of June, I remember that, and then we started heading south and then when the Third Army came in, and once I had relieved the others we got in and relieved the 101st Airborne.

George Pulakos Wounded

JOHN LONG: Did you ever wind up in St. Lo?

GEORGE PULAKOS: No. I ended up in Carentan. That is where I saw General Patton for the first time, and then at Carentan and here again I looked on maps but I could never orient myself, but I do remember we came to like a valley with hedgerows was all up it and you could look down in the valley and the Deers Canal was going through the bottom of that valley and we were to cross that valley and engage the enemy.

I wasn't supposed to go but the regiment lost their medic and I got transferred over there. I got through the Deers Canal and climbed across it and I was treating some wounded and then I got hit.

JOHN LONG: Where were you wounded?

GEORGE PULAKOS: I was wounded in the hand.

There was a fellow laying on the side of the canal and I had reached up and I had pulled his dog tags out to see about his shots and then I proceeded to cut his sleeve to give him medicine because he was complaining of how bad he hurt.

I lifted the sleeve and I was cutting the sleeve and one of those small 2.5 chemical mortars landed in his chest and went up by me and one piece took the finger off, entered here and came out the back.

That was the night I was wounded. I swam back to the other lieutenant that bandaged me up and I started heading back. Half way across the valley I thought, the war is over for you. My hand was all mangled up, so I stood up and started to walk and all of a sudden something knocked me down. I realized then that I wasn't out of the war, so I finished crawling and ended up in a field hospital.

When they were x-raying me they came back and said we got to take some more pictures because you got some strange things in your hand. We see mortar fragments and what looks like a can opener.

JOHN LONG: What?

GEORGE PULAKOS: Then I remembered that guy I was tending I had a little blade in my hand, just a little blade.

JOHN LONG: That little can opener?

GEORGE PULAKOS: I got the blade at home. I also have a can opener to show you where it came from.

JOHN LONG: That's a story right there.

GEORGE PULAKOS: Then they also looked and saw embedded down there was a copper jacketed shell filled with…. and that is what knocked me down coming across the field, so I got hit by a mortar fragment, a can opener and I had the bullet that had ricocheted. My hand to this day has got maybe 50 or 65 little metal particles all through it.

JOHN LONG: Did you get a ticket back to England or did you have to endure?

GEORGE PULAKOS: Nah, they bandaged me up and sent me back to a hospital in Oxford, England. There they told me that I was going to lose my hand and put a hook on it, so I resigned myself to that, so finally they sent me back to the states.

They sent me to Howard General Hospital in New York and there they told me they would probably send me to the nearest hospital that does amputations; and it happened to be near Lancaster and Harrisburg, so they loaded us on a train, I fell asleep and when I woke up and I looked and I asked the guy where are we and he said going through Washington DC and I said, oh no, I am supposed to go to Pennsylvania.

I ended up in a hospital in Tuscaloosa Alabama, Northington General Hospital.

JOHN LONG: Wait a minute. Let me get this straight. They told you they were going to send you to the best place to amputate…

GEORGE PULAKOS: Well, the nearest one that does amputations.

JOHN LONG: Was in Pennsylvania and then you woke up in DC?

GEORGE PULAKOS: I woke up on the train in Tuscaloosa Alabama. That was lucky. They didn't amputate.

Well, I got down there and there was a pair of Jewish doctors from the Jewish Hospital in New York City. They looked at me and said; you know you are going to lose your hand. I said yes. They said you are resigned to it, and I said yep. They said how about letting us try something, so they did seven surgical procedures on it, one every month for seven months and they saved the hand.

They took tendons out. I got scars up here where they took tendons, sliding fascia, and so it was lucky I ended up in Tuscaloosa Alabama.

JOHN LONG: You wound up not getting the hook, that's great.

GEORGE PULAKOS: I was very, very lucky.

JOHN LONG: Tell us a little bit more about the action part back in Normandy.

GEORGE PULAKOS: In recalling them some of them were funny instances, some of them were scary. The only person that I ever saw that I had met before was that tall guy that stepped off the landing craft. All of a sudden, we were maybe about six or seven miles from the canal they sent up replacements because they needed replacements; two young kids that were just out of high school had been in training with me at Camp Pickett and we had just moved into a field and the foxholes were there from where the Germans had abandoned them.

One foxhole was alongside of them and those two kids came up and they leaned against the hedgerow and they started getting shelling coming in and one jumped into one of the foxholes and it was booby trapped and it blew all three of them all to pieces. That is the only people that I knew that I saw killed.

JOHN LONG: That hurts.

GEORGE PULAKOS: I'll tell you. We had gone through basic together.

201

JOHN LONG: What about the French civilians that you encountered?

GEORGE PULAKOS: Well, I got a funny tale. When there was a little bit of a lull in the battle I went to a farmhouse. Up there in Normandy there were dairy cows, there were orchards, and a lot of apple trees and I got to talking with the farmer.

I would give him my coffee rations and he would give us a chicken, and I said to him, I bet you are glad to see the Americans and he looked at me and said, not really. I said, well that is not very nice, and he said, you know, when the French were running this country I had to get up and milk my cows and take care of my animals and then the Germans took over and I still had to milk my cows and do the apples, and now you are here, are you going to milk my cows? I said, well point well taken.

JOHN LONG: Doesn't make any difference who is running the country he's still got to milk the cows.

GEORGE PULAKOS: When you are doing something that they need your product it doesn't make any difference who is running it. It's all the same to him, he didn't care.

JOHN LONG: Approximately how long was your time in Normandy?

GEORGE PULAKOS: I went in on June 6th. I was wounded on July 17th. I got out of the hospital and got back in the states in November or December and then I got out of Tuscaloosa around October. I was sent over to Camp Crowder and I was discharged from Camp Crowder, medical discharge.

JOHN LONG: So while you were getting the multiple surgeries in Tuscaloosa the war came to an end?

GEORGE PULAKOS: For me yeah. Yes it did, I was home. What they would do is operate on me and I would

202

get a thirty day furlough to go home and recuperate and then I would come back and they would do the pre-surgery stuff and they would operate and I would go home for another thirty days.

I happened to be home when Germany surrendered but I wasn't home with Japan surrendered. When I got discharged from Camp Crowder it was November, exactly three years plus one day that I was in the service. I got one pay with longevity. After three years you go into longevity pay so I got one longevity pay. I was lucky to survive it.

Everything worked out for me awfully good. I am classified at 100 percent disabled so the government is paying me a pension. I have been fortunate enough to been in Eerie. Eerie has one of the finest VA Hospitals in the system. For me sometimes it looked like it was pretty bleak, but it all turned out for the good. I got, in spite of being a year in the hospital, it seemed bleak at the time but that was a million dollar wound.

JOHN LONG: What about when you did get discharged how was your homecoming with your family and reunion and so forth?

GEORGE PULAKOS: Well, I had been seeing them every other month, so it wasn't much of a real big reunion.

JOHN LONG: It wasn't like you had been gone and then just came home one day.

GEORGE PULAKOS: I hadn't been gone no two years or something, I had been home every other month, but when I ended up at Camp Crowder there were two young nurses over the ward. I was in the hospital ward as a patient and they were both lieutenants, but in those days nurses weren't allowed to start IVs. You had to have a doctor, but at Walter Reed we started IVs.

When I got on the ward with the girls I happened to walk by them one time and they looked puzzled and I said what's wrong, and she said we can't balance our narcotic register, and I said well maybe I can help you, so I sat down and helped them. Then when they found out I was a medic they had me going around giving shots.

One of the doctors asked me to start an IV, and they had never started them, so I started their IVs for them. When I got a discharge, here I am still a PFC and I got two lieutenants, nice looking nurses and we hitchhiked to Springfield Missouri and we had a grand two or three days and I spent all my discharge money and then I went home but I had two young ladies.

JOHN LONG: Did you do anything in particular after you got out in the way of a career?

GEORGE PULAKOS: No, like I said I eventually went to work for the medical company, Castle Sterilizer and American Sterilizer. I stayed with them for 30 years. I retired in 1987. I didn't retire for a long time.

JOHN LONG: How did your war time experiences affect your life and the way you look at life I suppose, and what life lessons did you learn?

GEORGE PULAKOS: All I know is that I am thankful the way it all turned out. Like I told you I was very lucky. I came out of it.

Then I got married. I married the best woman in the world. We were married for 62 years. She died in 2008. We had 62 years together, and then I came down here, I have a son here. If I could wish anybody anything I would wish you had a boy like him. He does everything for me. I am the happiest guy in the world right now. He is making my last years very nice.

JOHN LONG: Did you ever have any problems with like the PTSD aspect?

GEORGE PULAKOS: Exactly what are you asking me?

JOHN LONG: Well, you know nowadays…post traumatic stress disorder and all that.

GEORGE PULAKOS: The only thing that I have even come close happened about a year after. I happened to be thinking about the day I got hit and that mortar fragment hit him in the middle of his chest, about 18 inches from my head and I got the shakes.

JOHN LONG: That is called the survivor's syndrome.

GEORGE PULAKOS: I don't know what it is, but it lasted maybe one evening. I happened to be in the bed at the time. I thought, my God, how close that was.

JOHN LONG: Too close for comfort.

GEORGE PULAKOS: That is the only thing that I would say that even comes close. Other than that I am pretty well adjusted.

JOHN LONG: It has been a pleasure interviewing you.

Oscar Russell D-Day Experiences

I asked Oscar Russell what took place while you guys were waiting for the call to come for the invasion? What did you do, what kind of boat was it?

OSCAR RUSSELL: A little ole LCM (Landing Craft Mechanized). We had a bulldozer on it.

JOHN LONG: About how many guys were with you on it?

OSCAR RUSSELL: About 13 of us I think.

JOHN LONG: Who else was on this, did you carry a boat, a tank?

OSCAR RUSSELL: We carried, our little ole boat, they had made a ramp up at the front where the tanks and all could go off. On this little ramp that they had up there they had another little wood ramp that would raise that tank up high enough so it would shoot over the lip that dropped down, and they would shoot over that.

The men had a bulldozer blade in front of that tank and it was set up to where as soon as they moved those obstacles out of the way and made a road, cleared the path for it, that then he could drop that bulldozer blade.

JOHN LONG: Go back a little bit now to where you were getting ready to go into Normandy. Go back to where you got on the ship there in England. The boat you was on, did the sides let down?

OSCAR RUSSELL: Not the one we was on but the other boat...that we were pulling...

206

JOHN LONG: Okay, lets come back now to where you were getting ready.

OSCAR RUSSELL: The LCM. We had to tow that LCM and the weather had gotten so rough they just couldn't handle it so all the fellows got off. I think it was the demolition group, about 30 or 40.

JOHN LONG: Let me take you back a little. You are in England. You know you are going to do something, you don't know where you are going or what is going to happen. You loaded up with 13 guys with a tank on your ship. You know that you are getting ready for something to happen. Now, while you were getting ready for this to happen, what did you guys do there while you were still in England knowing that this D-Day was coming, on this night before? What did you do?

OSCAR RUSSELL: Some of them would shoot craps all night long. Some of them would do that, shoot craps, joke and all like that. I didn't do that.

JOHN LONG: And you said that you met this British guy, tell us about him. This is the night before you left out one morning and you had to turn around and come back.

OSCAR RUSSELL: That's right, and this ole British guy, he could tell some lies. His father would tease him and knock him down and everything else like that. We figured he was telling one. He said, you dirty yanks, when you hit the beach, he said, I will be standing up there waving you in. So, we made a big laugh out of that.

JOHN LONG: We will get to the beach a little bit later. So you left out of England and you headed for Normandy.

OSCAR RUSSELL: We were towing this LCM and it had the demolition crew and things on it. Those officers were just talking on those CBs and telephones and didn't realize that the Germans were hearing what they were saying; they

207

could pick up our radio. We couldn't go so they finally had to drop the anchor, so the anchor would pull us back so we wouldn't hit those big rocks there.

JOHN LONG: So you have to turn around? Did you go out on one day and have to come back because the weather was so bad?

OSCAR RUSSELL: Yeah.

JOHN LONG: Then you came back and had to start over? It's a historical fact that Eisenhower had to delay a full day because of the weather.

OSCAR RUSSELL: Right.

JOHN LONG: And almost didn't go the second, but he couldn't wait any longer.

OSCAR RUSSELL: Right.

JOHN LONG: Okay, so now you are coming in to where you landed, the demolition crew, and the guys from the LCM, what happened there?

OSCAR RUSSELL: We were there beside this British ship. The great Marine engines got sand in the filters, so we couldn't run our engines. We had to have electricity to cook food.

The British used coal to cook with, so we told them we had the food and they had the fire. We got us a fire axe and we chopped the storage bin was up front, it was on the right hand side I believe of that LCT so they took a chopping axe, or a fire axe and knocked a hole in it and got on the British ship.

When we went down to eat we come back up and the skipper's pearl handled knife and his pistol was missing and his cigarettes.

Well, we got this fellow that got up on top of that vent and he had a 45 pistol on him. We all carried a 45 pistol. He got to flipping it and telling them I will give you a certain time to get that stuff and get it back up here and we started.

He was shell-shocked you better watch him. So, boy it was coming. We went down and come back and all that stuff was right back where it should have been. So, we had a spell there.

Everybody had a little bit of money and they would put it together and buy stuff. It was there on the beach where you could go up into town and buy stuff that we needed. So our skipper, he liked to smoke, and we all got rid of all our money, or just a very little bit, we got down to about $8 or so was all he had and he said boys, he said I like to smoke. I am not going to spend my last money on you fellows.

Well we stayed on there and we just got up when we wanted to and sleep like we wanted to. Somebody would come by and wake us up.

JOHN LONG: And all the fighting was going on during all of this? All the tanks, the battleships, all the destroyers, everything was back behind you? Now, let's go back just a little bit. Let's go back to that LCM. When ya'll landed; first of all the tanks had to get out and move all those Germans?

OSCAR RUSSELL: Yeah.

JOHN LONG: During this time what was happening up on this cliff, where the bunkers and everything were up there. What was taking place up there?

OSCAR RUSSELL: Well, they were up there and would be in a little church steeple. See, they were just with those 88s. They were just picking these ships off. The Germans were doing this. But nobody really at first knew where it was coming from. Well, it was hemmed in so that we couldn't hit it, but there was a skipper that was either the Destroyer or the Destroyer Escort, and I don't see...it was just a God's miracle that he got between us and that thing and he started landing those bullets into that thing and he blew that thing up. That little church steeple up there; he kept laying into. I don't see how in the world he got around us with that Destroyer but he got around it anyway.

JOHN LONG: One thing that you told me when we talked on the phone was that you could actually see these gentlemen, these rangers trying to scale the cliffs with a rope.

OSCAR RUSSELL: Oh yeah, they were right there. You see, Ft. LoHo, all the other places that was out open, all right, the Germans already had those all built up. I mean they were really fortified. I guess they didn't figure that the Americans would try that way. They had all behind there fixed up with these things that gliders would come in and they would hit those things with the gliders.

JOHN LONG: It sounds to me like they were going to rely on the cliffs for protection and they didn't have to fortify that area as much.

OSCAR RUSSELL: Right, they just didn't even have the idea probably that they would try climbing it. But those places were just out pretty close to the beach. I got a lot of little things that shows the things on it. They didn't figure that that place would be hit. You see, this was.... there, it was open like.... down here. There was an opening to get through, and I don't think that they figured.... they had that fortified so good they didn't figure we could get through in there. They had no idea the Americans would try to go up those cliffs.

JOHN LONG: I think it is fairly accurate that there were 300 rangers assigned to that rough spot where the cliff was and only 90 survived. In other words, 210 didn't make it.

OSCAR RUSSELL: That sounds good. You see, when they would stick their heads up they would shoot them. They would see their heads coming up and they were shooting those rangers off as they stuck their heads up when they got to the top of the cliff, they would shoot them.

JOHN LONG: I am still trying to find out, what happened to these guys in the LCM that you were pulling. Did they all live; were they killed by the Germans? The LCM you were pulling. Did they all make it to the beach?

OSCAR RUSSELL: We got on the LCM. See our boat couldn't make it anymore.

JOHN LONG: But you got to the beach? Got through the obstacles? Was anybody killed or anything?

OSCAR RUSSELL: Not any of our men.

JOHN LONG: But what about the other men ya'll were delivering?

OSCAR RUSSELL: The demolition group and all of them they got killed.

JOHN LONG: How did they get killed?

OSCAR RUSSELL: Trying to get in. Some of the tanks that they mined trying to go in where we were, they had a rubber thing around it to try to make it float, but the thing about it the water was so rough, the water would just slosh over into those tanks and began to drown those guys.

I didn't know it until later on that I was supposed to be in a medical group.

JOHN LONG: So they forgot to tell you about that?

OSCAR RUSSELL: Yeah, Fox 29 was the medical group.

JOHN LONG: Okay, so back to this guy that was in this tank. The tank was in the front of the boat, did he get off the boat and into the water? What was he supposed to do?

OSCAR RUSSELL: He got off into the water and he started removing those obstacles there, pushing those obstacles off. It had a bulldozer blade in front of it, and so he could take those bulldozer blades and push those things back out of the way so that it would make a road for these others to pull in and let the troops off and they could back up and get out of the way and let some more come in, and see they had to have it to where these boats that could go in and then be able to back right out or either make another little circle where they could run in and then back right out like that.

JOHN LONG: With regards to what we discussed before we started recording, do you have a perception of how you felt during all this, all of this was going on that you have been describing. Did you have any fear, or was you kind of like me when I was over there. I was so young I didn't care what happened type thing. I knew things were going to happen but you got no control over it.

OSCAR RUSSELL: You know, people might think I am a little bit crazy, but I don't think I ever really...I had concerns, but I don't think I ever really had any fear. I knew that my mother and the people at the little church where I grew up, I knew that they were praying for me. I knew that my mother was on her knees every night praying for me and the other two boys, and so I really just really don't think I ever had any real fear; concern yes. Everybody wants to live but then I knew I had a job to do and that's what the Lord wanted me to do and everything would be all right.

JOHN LONG: Looking back now, in the hindsight, like they call 20-20, looking back, and since we are trying to gather information in the twilight time of this particular historical event, is there something you feel inside that you would like to leave for the future generations about wars, about your experiences, and about how all that developed. Is there something you would like to say for the record, maybe for your grandkids sake and so forth?

OSCAR RUSSELL: Well, I think the best thing I could say to them is put yourself in the Lord's hands and pray that you will be in God's will; whatever He sees fit.

Percy Scarborough D-Day Experiences

JOHN LONG: You were there when they said it was time to go and then they postponed it a day.

PERCY SCARBOROUGH: Well, what we had been doing, about two weeks, three weeks prior to this every night we were on alert and we had to sleep with our pack and everything, packed up, your clothes on, you are on full alert and they come in and they would pick us up and put us in these trucks, and at that time we moved down to Plymouth England and go out on the beach there and just sit there.

The trucks would leave and in an hour or so they would come back and pick us up and carry us back. This particular day they came and got us that night rather, they came and got us, but that day they fed us and when they fed us they gave us apples and oranges which was a rare thing, and a Coca-Cola, hot Coca-Cola, and I told some of the boys that something was fixing to happen, it's going.

When we got on the trucks that night to go down to the beach they unloaded us and in about forty-five minutes I saw a big speck out there on the water coming in. I said boys, this is it. We ain't going back this time, and sure enough they loaded us on LSTs and moved us out in the channel and we boarded a liberty ship there.

We went down the English Channel all day that morning and all day down the English Channel to just before dark it made a U-turn and started back up the English Channel and that's when, I guess they got the go ahead for the invasion, but we were all on ships ready to go.

JOHN LONG: It sounds like they was kind of moving you in and out, in and out, so maybe nobody knew what day it was going to be.

PERCY SCARBOROUGH: That's the whole thing nobody knew when. We didn't know what was taking place really. In fact we were listening to Berlin Bessie, you might have heard that name before, she was a commentator for the Germans on the radio and she could tell us more about what was going on than we could get from our own side.

In fact, she was telling us when we were moving down the channel that day that we would be going to southern France to make an invasion, that's where they thought we were going. She knew we were on the ships because she called some by names of the outfits. They had some good intelligence for sure. We all really thought that's where we were going to cause we had been listening to her.

JOHN LONG: And she had been telling some pretty straight stuff.

PERCY SCARBOROUGH: Pretty straight stuff.

JOHN LONG: Tell us about when they actually decided to go into Normandy.

PERCY SCARBOROUGH: They told us about 3 o'clock that morning.

JOHN LONG: Did they name the beach or did they just say we are going in?

PERCY SCARBOROUGH: They just said we were making an invasion. We didn't know if it was on Omaha or Utah, we didn't know what it was; we just knew we were headed in. Of course, we lost probably half of our outfit.

JOHN LONG: On the beach or in the water?

PERCY SCARBOROUGH: Both. They were shelling so bad and all that the LSTs wouldn't carry us in. They dropped us out where it was over our heads and we were out there bobbling. We had base plates and tripods on our back loaded down and when they dropped you over your head we lost a lot of people out there.

JOHN LONG: A lot of guys drown?

PERCY SCARBOROUGH: And if they didn't drown they lost their equipment, a lot of them. They didn't have any equipment.

JOHN LONG: Do you recall some instances of, one fellow said they even weighted down some of the LSTs off the ships too heavy and they sunk right there off the big ships when they got into the landing crafts.

PERCY SCARBOROUGH: I didn't see any of that because we were scrambling and they were firing and we were firing back, the ships were firing back. I would doubt that happening because they had assigned so many people to each ship, now it could have happened; I am not saying it didn't happen.

JOHN LONG: But it didn't happen on your watch?

PERCY SCARBOROUGH: No.

JOHN LONG: Do you remember how you got out of the landing craft on the beach?

PERCY SCARBOROUGH: In the water. I mean when they let that gate down you had to get out.

JOHN LONG: So you come out of the gate. Was the water over your head right there?

PERCY SCARBOROUGH: Yeah.

JOHN LONG: How was you able to get to the beach?

PERCY SCARBOROUGH: I don't know. I don't even know. Of course, I was probably one of the smallest men there. My height wasn't but about 5'6" then and weighed down too and all, all I was doing was I was scrambling trying to get to a place where I could get my head above water.

JOHN LONG: Did you have a floatation device or something?

PERCY SCARBOROUGH: No. We didn't have anything, but we had our full field pack and of course I carried a tripod. It weighed 46 pounds, the tripod itself.

JOHN LONG: What's your first recollection that you want to tell me about, after you got on the beach and what happened.

PERCY SCARBOROUGH: Take cover. As quick as I could take cover I took cover and I stayed in cover practically all day that day of the invasion. I understand they said we were so many miles inland, and that night we were still on the beach. We spent three nights on the beach before we were able to get up and come up on land.

JOHN LONG: If I understand it right from our previous conversation, the best you could tell you were on the right flank of Omaha Beach? Do you remember St. Lo?

216

PERCY SCARBOROUGH: Yeah.

JOHN LONG: Going into St. Lo?

PERCY SCARBOROUGH: Like millions of times. Of course, I pronounce it a little different than they do.

JOHN LONG: How do you say that one? I know St. Lo, but how do you say the other one?

PERCY SCARBOROUGH: There were two little towns or communities there, and the Germans had it all blocked and when we broke through there that's when we really; Patton broke high in St. Lo.

JOHN LONG: He did get to come in up there?

PERCY SCARBOROUGH: Yeah.

JOHN LONG: Tell me about that aspect of it; when he showed up and what happened.

PERCY SCARBOROUGH: Of course I was with the First Army up until that time and they transferred us back because we didn't know we were being transferred. We were told later that we were back in the Third Army, but when Patton came in we seemed to make some headway. We were making very little headway with the hedgerows.

JOHN LONG: The hedgerows were something else to. I have always wandered why there wasn't more preparations for the hedgerows, because the hedgerows presented a problem that it didn't seem like everybody was prepared for. Did they tell you anything in advance that there was going to be a problem with hedgerows or anything like that?

PERCY SCARBOROUGH: Nothing.

JOHN LONG: Nothing was said about hedgerows, and it was a problem.

PERCY SCARBOROUGH: A tremendous problem.

JOHN LONG: How did your outfit negotiate the hedgerow problem?

PERCY SCARBOROUGH: We would just hold on to them and climb over them, it just like a fence more or less. It was dirt and hedges around them. Of course there was an opening that you could get in there, if you could get to that opening. Of course, the Germans had snipers in the trees shooting at us, against the hedgerows and us trying to go over it because the tanks couldn't manipulate the hedgerows.

JOHN LONG: Where was you when Patton's outfit came in...Patton? Was you still up there around St. Lo?

PERCY SCARBOROUGH: Yeah, back towards Cherbourg probably St. Lo. I am just guessing, probably 10 miles back, 5 miles back from St. Lo whenever he came in.

JOHN LONG: Was that to the north of St. Lo or back towards the southern part because St. Lo is setting kind of in that curve and up at the top is where Cherbourg is; was ya'll between St. Lo and Cherbourg?

PERCY SCARBOROUGH: Yeah. Now they told us Cherbourg was back that a way. We had no earthly idea what Cherbourg was even, other than a name at that time, and of course maps that they gave our company the map didn't take in a mile each way we didn't know what the other part was.

JOHN LONG: Sounds like they just gave you a map of where you were supposed to go.

PERCY SCARBOROUGH: That's all. They gave us an objective to take and gave you the map that had that objective on the map.

JOHN LONG: Do you remember the specific objective that you are talking about there, as far as, you know it was a narrow strip, and you said it was for the objective, was there a specific objective? Like, you have to take this little town for example.

PERCY SCARBOROUGH: They didn't mention towns. Town were not mentioned. It would show up on the map that we got but they never mentioned towns.

JOHN LONG: Was there some sort of like the pill boxes and things? Would that be an objective?

PERCY SCARBOROUGH: Pill boxes and certain areas that they wanted, like an intersection of a road or take this road and hold it to where they could bring supplies through, that type. I didn't realize at that time but I have seen pictures of it since then a lot of the area was flooded there. Of course we thought it was normal, a swamp, but they flooded it.

JOHN LONG: You didn't happen to see that documentary about Graignes where they dropped paratroopers into the swamp and they were off course, the worse drop of the whole thing?

PERCY SCARBOROUGH: They dropped paratroopers ahead of us on Omaha and they were wandering around back behind enemy lines and we had, you ever seen these little Cracker Jack boxes that had snappers in them?

JOHN LONG: You talking about a cricket?

PERCY SCARBOROUGH: Cricket.

JOHN LONG: I have a picture of one over there in my iphone. Did ya'll have them too?

PERCY SCARBOROUGH: We had them, and the paratrooper had them and every day they changed our code and changed the paratrooper's codes.

JOHN LONG: The number of clicks?

PERCY SCARBOROUGH: The number of clicks, and if you heard a click, and your click was a two you better answer it with a two.

JOHN LONG: The same type click?

PERCY SCARBOROUGH: Same type thing, it was a cricket answering a cricket, but now if you answered it different than what...

JOHN LONG: I can see where changing the code everyday would be...some people don't get the word you know to change the click.

PERCY SCARBOROUGH: A lot of that happened. In fact, the thing that bothered me more than anything else, I think, was going; maybe we would go up, I can't think of the name of it, and they would bring us back in a day or so and move around to another area and all the people in my outfit had a tent over it and you would see all the boys stacked up on side of the road like cord wood waiting for the burial detail to come by and pick them up. I think that bothered me most.

JOHN LONG: Total number of days that you were involved with the actual Normandy aspect of the invasion. About how long was you up there?

PERCY SCARBOROUGH: Not knowing exactly where Normandy ended at, I don't know. I can tell you about how many days I was there in the vicinity.

JOHN LONG: In the vicinity, that's what I am asking.

PERCY SCARBOROUGH: I would say it was probably August to September, somewhere along in there.

JOHN LONG: Did you go into Paris?

PERCY SCARBOROUGH: No, they wouldn't let our outfit go into Paris. They said we would tear it up too bad. They turned us south of it.

JOHN LONG: And made ya'll go around?

PERCY SCARBOROUGH: They did. All our infantry boys shot from the hip. I never seen it. They shot from the hip with their M1s. That's the way they shot. In fact the German Berlin Bessie called our outfit the E-lite Division.

JOHN LONG: Instead of Elite, E-lite. She didn't know how to say it did she?

PERCY SCARBOROUGH: Really when we started moving was when we broke through in St. Lo. We started taking ground then; ground that we were looking at more than anything else.

JOHN LONG: Is there any particular instance that you remember that's kind of on the humorous side? For example, I had one fellow tell me that he was down behind this personnel carrier in St. Lo and the Germans shot an armored piercing shell right through that personnel carrier and hit at his feet. He looked up and there were five guys coming out of there all bloody, except they weren't bloody, that thing had hit the hydraulic fluid thing and put that red hydraulic fluid all over them and they didn't have a scratch on them.

PERCY SCARBOROUGH: The only thing that I thought was a little funny, we had moved into this hedgerow after dark, sometime around 10 or 11 o'clock that night.

We snuck into this area and dug our foxholes and everything and sometime during the night I had to come out of my foxhole and go use the bathroom and when I reached up to pull myself out of the foxhole I felt a hand, and it was cold. The next morning when daylight came it was a German soldier killed right there.

JOHN LONG: By your foxhole?

PERCY SCARBOROUGH: By my foxhole. Of course it was night and we were digging in and I didn't know nothing about it until I started out of that hole.

JOHN LONG: Well when you dug the foxhole he wasn't there was he?

PERCY SCARBOROUGH: Yeah, he was dead there.

JOHN LONG: No, I am talking about when you prepared the foxhole. That happened …. He got shot and killed right there by your foxhole that night.

PERCY SCARBOROUGH: Sometime or another.

JOHN LONG: After you dug the foxhole?

PERCY SCARBOROUGH: I don't really know whether he was there before. One of those peculiar things.

JOHN LONG: That was an unusual thing. And you didn't even get out of that foxhole until you touched that cold hand.

PERCY SCARBOROUGH: And you dug in just as quick as you could and stayed there, cause when daylight come you never knew whenever you were going to have snipers all the way around you in them trees around the hedgerows.

JOHN LONG: Have you got any other thoughts about that particular point in time you would like to mention?

PERCY SCARBOROUGH: I don't know where this took place at; when we met the English there, I don't know exactly where it was at. It was what was called the Argentan-Falaise Gap.

It was just a valley like and the English were over there and we were over there and the German Army was trying to escape through them and this truck we had it pinned down with mortar there and we would see the Germans get out of the ditch and they would try to make it back to the truck and we would fire on them and they would get back in the ditch, so we finally just went ahead and did away with them and after things quieted down.

I told a buddy of mine, which we were kind of scavengers anyway looking, I said something was in that truck they were trying to get back to, I said let's ease down there and find out what it was.

It was a German payroll, French currency, a little over a million dollars, fresh printed I mean.

We got a little of it home, very little of it, and they found out where it was coming from and of course they threatened to court martial us if we didn't turn it in, so we turned it in to them. I don't know whether that was in Normandy or further down. I think it was further down; I am not sure because it wasn't a whole lot between Omaha and Paris down here.

JOHN LONG: As a matter of fact you can drive from Paris to Omaha Beach in about an hour and a half.

PERCY SCARBOROUGH: Like I said, it wasn't too much. Not like you had too much to do with other than fight, but they were smart people. The Germans were smart people. They had a tank and 45s as well.

JOHN LONG: You got to hand it to them. They wasn't acting foolish, they knew what they were doing.

PERCY SCARBOROUGH: They knew well what they were doing. We lost a lot of men there; boys, young boys.

JOHN LONG: Here is something a little different here they was asking questions about. Did you write home a lot? In other words, did you keep in touch pretty good?

PERCY SCARBOROUGH: Quite a bit, but not a whole lot because you didn't have the time. You didn't have the necessary materials to do it. In fact, the first bath, we went 43 days without a bath.

JOHN LONG: 43 days between baths?

PERCY SCARBOROUGH: Well we washed off with our helmet ...

JOHN LONG: You did the best you could but you didn't have a shower in other words.

PERCY SCARBOROUGH: We were on the edge of a river, a small river, not a big river, a stream you might say and built a portable shower tent thing.

JOHN LONG: But that was about 43 days?

PERCY SCARBOROUGH: 43 days. I said I am going to stay in that shower for two hours. They had a big ole First Sergeant out there; I bet he weighed 300 pounds, big guy. He said okay, I am going to tell you how it's going to be. When you go in this end down here pull all your clothes off and leave them.

We are going to issue you new clothes when you come out the other end. He said you got one minute to get your clothes off, you got three minutes under the shower, you got one minute out. Five minutes is all we had to strip, get a shower and get out the other end.

JOHN LONG: So your idea about staying along time under the shower didn't work.

PERCY SCARBOROUGH: It didn't work at all. I wasn't about to try to buck him. He looked like he could whoop the Army himself, and probably would have if you would have tried him. Of course, if we hit a stream or something we would wash off, bathe, and jump in it and do the best we could. Of course, we were issued, every day we were issued clean socks and clean under wear every day. Most of the time, sometime we weren't, but most of the time. That's what they tried to do.

JOHN LONG: They tried their best to keep you in underwear and socks knowing you couldn't take a bath. Looking back now it seems like there was pretty good preparations made for what happened. In other words, it was a pretty decent planned operation.

PERCY SCARBOROUGH: It was a great plan; for that many men and that much equipment. You can not believe the amount of equipment that come in there.

JOHN LONG: What about the number of ships in the channel and the number of planes overhead.

PERCY SCARBOROUGH: I have no idea how many there was.

JOHN LONG: But there was plenty wasn't there?

PERCY SCARBOROUGH: There was. All you could see was the sky light up. They were firing from about 12 o'clock that night all the way on and the planes going over, the sky would be lit up with planes going across. It was unreal. They had that very well planned. In fact, I don't think they could have planned it any better.

JOHN LONG: Here's one. You might have already told me about it, but what was your worse moment, the worse thing you had to plant it somewhere else, what sticks out in your mind that was the worse experience that you encountered while you were in Normandy?

PERCY SCARBOROUGH: You know, I don't know whether it was in Normandy or where it was at. I can't recall exactly where it was at. No, it wasn't in Normandy because I was sick with a cold and we got out of Normandy before winter came so it would have been later.

Percy Scarborough at Battle of the Bulge

JOHN LONG: Was you in the Battle of the Bulge? That may have been about where it was.

PERCY SCARBOROUGH: This forward observation guy, he was from Plymouth Falls Oregon. Me and him switched off; off and on. I would relieve him. He was the regular observation guy and I would relieve him and it was my time to go up with the rifle boys and I was sick with a cold and I had gone in the basement of this house and I had thrown my raincoat down on a sweet beet pile.

They had sweet beets like big ole turnips or rutabagas and such, and I had gone to sleep. They come in looking for me and one of my people there told them he is just sick with a cold and my buddy said well I will go back, ain't no problem and about twenty minutes later I woke up and my buddy had been killed.

JOHN LONG: The one from Plymouth Falls?

PERCY SCARBOROUGH: We had a 240 and artillery came in short and we had 18 rifle boys, were my men there in this ole barn like thing out on the edge of this little town like thing and this thing came in short and got them all.

JOHN LONG: Was it our own...was it friendly fire that came in short? In other words it was our fire, but it fell short?

PERCY SCARBOROUGH: And I was supposed to be out there.

JOHN LONG: You would have been out there if you hadn't had that cold?

PERCY SCARBOROUGH: In fact, three or four days later I had to go back for one day in the hospital and get some shots and stuff.

JOHN LONG: Let me just ask you; are you OK with us talking about this?

PERCY SCARBOROUGH: I have never really talked about it.

JOHN LONG: I know sir. I wished everybody that I have been able to interview had never told me before but some of them had told their story and then some of them had their story told when they applied for the French Medal that I told you about, but I can see when you, when you got through with it you just came home and then what?

PERCY SCARBOROUGH: That's it.

JOHN LONG: After you got home and out of the military did you have any trouble from your experiences in the war?

PERCY SCARBOROUGH: Quite a bit yeah, but of course I was real fortunate when I was over there, I was single. The day I came home, well I came home at night; I got home about 11 o'clock at night to a little community out from Meridian.

JOHN LONG: Near Meridian?

PERCY SCARBOROUGH: Yeah, just out of Meridian about six miles, but that's where my Daddy lived at that time. They didn't know I was anywhere around and I came home and my sister worked at a cleaners there in Meridian and I went out the next morning, well the next day about lunch time to see her and this young lady was in there with her, working with her, and I met her and I kind of liked the ole gal but it took me about two months to get her to go out with me.

JOHN LONG: And she worked there with your sister at the cleaners?

PERCY SCARBOROUGH: Yeah, I met my wife the day I came out of service, well the next day, and we were married about a year, or a little over a year later and have been married for 65 years, I can't remember, maybe 66 or 67.

JOHN LONG: You didn't get wounded any?

PERCY SCARBOROUGH: No. I stuck my leg out a million times hoping I would get wounded where I could go back but I didn't have guts enough to hold it out there, I would jerk it back.

JOHN LONG: So, you would think one minute you want to go home and then the next nah I don't want to do it that way. (Laugh) What did you do after you got married and settled down and everything? What kind of work did you do to make a living?

PERCY SCARBOROUGH: My first job was an auto parts business. I worked for an auto parts company for about two or three years and then I worked for an automobile finance company, ran the office for them for about two or three years, and then worked for a glass company and finally went in the glass business and stayed in it about fifteen years and then I went in the trucking business and been in it off and on ever since.

JOHN LONG: You the only fellow I have interviewed that's still working.

PERCY SCARBOROUGH: Is that right?

JOHN LONG: Yes, sir. Everybody else is 88 and 90 years old. You are 88 years old and you still sitting in the office.

PERCY SCARBOROUGH: I will be working till they put me in the ground, if I'm able.

JOHN LONG: Why not?

PERCY SCARBOROUGH: Well, my wife has Alzheimer's and she fell and broke her hip and pelvis and I have to have someone come and sit with her before I can leave. I enjoy working; that's all I have ever known. I came up during the depression.

JOHN LONG: I think you guys, being part of The Greatest Generation were molded because of the depression, the toughness and the ability to get the job done.

PERCY SCARBOROUGH: A nickel was a nickel. I remember when the cokes went from four cents to a nickel and I said I will never pay a nickel for a coke.

JOHN LONG: You never thought you were going to get a hot one over there in England either did you?

PERCY SCARBOROUGH: That's kind of hard to take though, a hot coke. And of course the reason we didn't go a lot of places in England, you know as a soldier, we were not first class citizens over there. Back then we were considered second class. If we rode the train or anything we was in second class, we never got first class or anything.

JOHN LONG: The British got first class.

PERCY SCARBOROUGH: Some British did, now some British didn't.

JOHN LONG: They liked to single you out.

PERCY SCARBOROUGH: They separated us and if you went to a pub there were certain pubs that we couldn't...that were off limits to us.

JOHN LONG: Probably didn't like you and didn't want you is why it was off limits.

PERCY SCARBOROUGH: They didn't want us messing with their women, but you know the worse town; you know the English were real good at how they withstood what they withstood.

JOHN LONG: They had been bombed pretty heavy before ya'll got there.

PERCY SCARBOROUGH: Plymouth England did not have a building standing, of course that was right on the coast there, the channel there. It did not have a building standing that I ever saw there.

JOHN LONG: That in and of itself would be a pretty sobering experience to go to a country knowing you were fixing to go see about why and then that country had all that destruction in it and ya'll were fixing to give it back to them.

PERCY SCARBOROUGH: They were strong willed. The English were strong willed people. We would set on, of course we were on the highest hill in England and bombs they come over us and set off right over the top of us, or it would sound like it anyway and we could tell they were headed down to explode, but they didn't have any sights or anything like that on them, they just had so much fuel in them, and of course in Metz France there, that's where they had the big tom gun that they moved out of that mountainside there on a railroad car and shot it and we were in a holding position right straight across from that.

JOHN LONG: And that was over Metz?

PERCY SCARBOROUGH: Metz France. The old boy that was set up right next to me with a 50 caliber machine gun that would come on over here, and of course what could it do to big tom? It couldn't even break a rail or anything, but he somehow, I don't know how he let it happen but he got a box of tracer bullets in his gun and as they rolled that thing out he started with this machine gun and all and traced it right back to us.

Of course they didn't shoot the big Tommy gun at us; they couldn't because it was too big. They shot it miles and miles away but that didn't keep them from putting artillery on our rear ends.

JOHN LONG: If I understand that part correct, the fellow put the tracer bullets in there not knowing it was a box of tracer bullets, and all that did was tell them where you were at.

PERCY SCARBOROUGH: Exactly where we were at. They busted our rumps.

JOHN LONG: And it didn't take them long either did it?

PERCY SCARBOROUGH: No sir. Little things like that happened. I tell you another thing we did, we would fire all night long, we would capture an ammunition gun that the Germans had, I guess it was an 81, it looked like ours. We could never get the sights to work out; we would just shoot it for random fire.

JOHN LONG: The ammo was interchangeable, but the sights wasn't?

PERCY SCARBOROUGH: We captured the guns and all, and we got our company commander to let us fire at night at will, and we were throwing the German rounds back at them with their own mortar weapon.

I was on the roof of this house right on the banks and it had a glass panes in the roof, had about three or four panes in the roof that you could go up in the attic and look out, so we were looking out at these Germans right across the river there dug in and this ole German, he would get up and ease out, he would take two or three steps out and go back and I told my buddy that was up there with me, I said he's got to go out to use the bathroom and we let him fool around there for about thirty minutes and he finally got nerve enough to go, and I let him get all set up and I called mortar fire on his butt.

JOHN LONG: While he was hunkered down?

PERCY SCARBOROUGH: Yeah, and I hated that after that, but I knew he was getting some relief, bound to have been hurting, bad.

JOHN LONG: He wasn't coming out of that foxhole?

PERCY SCARBOROUGH: No, he wasn't coming out of that joker. We found all kinds of ways to implement, like the rifle boys would be hold up down here in this house and we could go up in the roof of this house and they would have little square panes of glass in there and we could look over and see what was going on with our field glasses and then call for fire. We were just crazy enough and didn't have sense enough to know it was dangerous as hell. We would just hang on and didn't have a worry in the world really. We would call for fire up there. You couldn't get nobody else to go up there because of the action. They would zero in on them old houses. That's where they figured we were at. Most of the time they would be in the basement or somewhere like that.

JOHN LONG: I guess common sense would tell you that you would be better off in a basement than somewhere on a roof looking out a window on a roof, but like you said when you are young like that you don't think about that very much.

PERCY SCARBOROUGH: You know, we ate good over there, we had sausage and bacon and ham and plenty of potatoes.

JOHN LONG: Potato schnapps?

PERCY SCARBOROUGH: That's what they had most over there.

JOHN LONG: I drank schnapps when I was over there, I didn't like it.

PERCY SCARBOROUGH: It's good with orange juice, not orange juice but grapefruit juice.

JOHN LONG: So you had to cut it with grapefruit juice?

PERCY SCARBOROUGH: We had a five gallon jug on the trailer, on the ammunition trailer. We kept a five gallon jug of it.

JOHN LONG: Just in case you came across some schnapps?

PERCY SCARBOROUGH: We had some.

JOHN LONG: In other words, you just kept it with you? The company commander didn't pay any attention to that?

PERCY SCARBOROUGH: He didn't even know it. I got, well it was right before Christmas when we were in a holding position we got in a new company commander, which was a Second Lieutenant, everybody else would get killed or get wounded and we got this Second Lieutenant and I was going up to meet him to see who he was and what kind of guy he was, so I walked up.

He was in this old house that he called his office and I just walked in, and I was loaded with potato schnapps anyway, and he said soldier don't you know how to knock. I said hell yeah.

I went over to that door and closed it and took my foot and knocked it in and walked up and took that 45 and put it right to his head and I told him, you SOB you won't be here long because I am going to blow your brains out if you pull this kind of crap again.

We are all boys here, all together. Get that dang insignia off your shoulder because they are going to gump your ass. That's the reason I stay a PFC.

JOHN LONG: Did he write you up or something?

PERCY SCARBOROUGH: Didn't. First Sergeant wouldn't let him. He said you leave that boy alone and he did. He was there about two weeks; he got wounded when

233

we lost hundreds of them. I shouldn't have done it, I know I shouldn't have done it, but you know…

JOHN LONG: Well at the time, under them circumstances that's understandable.

PERCY SCARBOROUGH: At that same place, we went in a building right down below him there and the Germans had dug a big ole trench, like a foxhole to guard the town, and we were pulling guard there, we had two on and two off, and the windows were all knocked out the little house. We had a little ole half tent over the windows and a boy came in that night and he woke me up.

He said it's your time for guard duty, so I said okay. I got up, I carried a 45 and a carbine all the time and I just took the carbine and threw it over my shoulder and I had my overcoat and put it on and then I put my rifle on and I just pulled that tent back and took my hand and took a hand spring out the window because we had about a three foot snow bank out this ole window and out comes a German, that damn close.

JOHN LONG: Right out the window?

PERCY SCARBOROUGH: Right out the window. He was standing out there trying to give himself up, he said comrade, well I knew he was trying to give himself up, but I tell you what I could count every hair on my head that stood up.

JOHN LONG: Scared you a little bit?

PERCY SCARBOROUGH: Scared me, I wasn't expecting it, had no thoughts of one a being there and I just threw a hand spring out there and damn there he was.

JOHN LONG: You didn't know what he was fixing to do.

PERCY SCARBOROUGH: I had no idea until he said comrade, but it still didn't keep the hair from standing up on my head.

JOHN LONG: I understand that. Well, did he give himself up, turn him in?

PERCY SCARBOROUGH: Oh yeah we took him in, but you know there for a long time we wouldn't take prisoners.

JOHN LONG: Didn't have time to take them?

PERCY SCARBOROUGH: What you gonna do with them when they surrendered? You didn't have time to fool with them. The worse thing is what they told us, if you could wound one you are better off than killing him.

JOHN LONG: Cause he had to have somebody helping him.

PERCY SCARBOROUGH: He had to have at least two helping him, and that tied up three. It was an experience that I would never want to go back through it, but being through it and out it was an experience.

JOHN LONG: It had to be a life altering experience.

PERCY SCARBOROUGH: It was.

JOHN LONG: Was there any particular lessons that you think you learned as part of that, or being in that type of experience; life lessons type thing?

PERCY SCARBOROUGH: I could see that they were 100 years behind us and we had a great opportunity and I would have to send some of the industrial stuff over there that I saw in order to make a better situation for them; what I saw. I quit school when I was in the 10th grade.

JOHN LONG: You never did finish?

PERCY SCARBOROUGH: Yes, sir when I came out of service and got married I went to finish high school and strangely enough we couldn't get a college to open up around Meridian there I drove every night to Scooba, from Meridian to Scooba every night to college there for three months until we could get Meridian Junior College to open their doors at night so we could go to school at night there.

JOHN LONG: So you actually got some college in?

PERCY SCARBOROUGH: I got two years junior college in at night

JOHN LONG: Starting in Scooba and then switching to…

PERCY SCARBOROUGH: Then transferring to Meridian. That was back whenever it was all two lane. I will never forget how I got to be good friends with Mr. Buse there, he had a store there where you turned in the school, he and his wife did, and we would always run in there at night.

JOHN LONG: Did they call that East Mississippi Junior College back then?

PERCY SCARBOROUGH: No. East Mississippi Junior College back then was in Decatur. That was Scooba Junior College. I don't know what it's called now.

The War Ends

By April Germany faced its last days with 1.9 million German soldiers in the East fighting 6.4 million Russian soldiers and 1 million German soldiers in the West fighting 4 million Western Allied soldiers.

General Patton had wanted to be the first into Berlin. But Stalin had successfully lobbied for Eastern Germany to fall within the Soviet "sphere of influence" at the Big Three meeting in Yalta, so no plans were made by the Western Allies to seize the city by a ground operation.

The Russians reached the Berlin capital on April 21st. Hitler and his just married Eva Braun committed suicide on the 30th of April. The Russians found their remains which had been burned at Hitler's directive.

This was just two days after Mussolini had been captured and hanged by Italian partisans.

Germany surrendered unconditionally on 7 May and May 8 was declared and celebrated as VE (Victory in Europe) day.

The war in Europe was over.

President Truman's use of the atomic bomb in Japan resulted in their surrendered on August 14.

World War II was the biggest conflict in history in terms of people and areas involved; it lasted almost six years.

About 100 million people had been militarized and about 50 million had been killed; 15 million were soldiers, 20 million were Russian civilians, six million were Jews and over four million were Poles.

Chapter 5

The Horrors

As we write about memories of World War II we recognize that the most lasting memory is of the horrors of Hitler's camps. There had been rumors of Jews being slaughtered for several years however most could not believe such horrors to be true.

The scale and horrors of Hitler's program became very clear as more and more camps were liberated.

Perhaps we should not have been so surprised by Hitler's actions against the Jews. In his book *Mein Kampf* (My Struggle) which Hitler wrote in 1923-24, he clearly expresses his views on Jews. He says that they are the "source of all evil". And he discusses the need to eliminate all inferior and undesirable peoples to preserve the "Aryan" race.

Hitler took actions described in his book and established the first concentration camp at Dachau March 20, 1933, just five weeks after he took power as German chancellor. Dachau was situated on the outskirts of the town of Dachau, about 10 miles northwest of Munich.

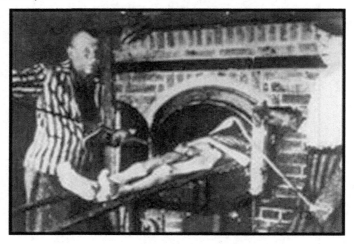

Dachau was the training center for SS concentration camp guards and was the model for other Nazi concentration camps.

Dachau prisoners were used as forced laborers to first build the camp and then for production of German armaments.

To increase war production the main camp was supplemented by dozens of satellite camps established near armaments factories in southern Germany and Austria. These camps were administered by the main camp and collectively called Dachau.

Dachau was also the first Nazi camp to use prisoners as human guinea pigs in medical experiments.

Doctor Josef Mengele became the world's most infamous doctor by leading the experiments on humans from his position of Chief Camp Physician at the Auschwitz concentration camp.

Dr. Mengele at Auschwitz and Argentina

Dr. Mengele fled Germany after the war and went to Argentina. He had avoided trial at the Nazi Doctor's Trial at Nuremberg when the US military released him by mistake.

He continued his medical and "experimental" practices in Argentina, Paraguay, and Brazil.

He lived a comfortable life until 1979 when he drowned while having a stroke. He died believing he had done the world and the superior races a favor with findings from his experiments.

***

When the American soldiers liberated Dachau they found 30 railroad cars just outside the camp. They were filled with bodies in various states of decomposition.

Inside the camp they found more bodies and 30,000 severely emaciated survivors.

Some of the American troops who liberated Dachau were so appalled by conditions at the camp that they machine-gunned at least 30 SS guards and most likely 10 times this official report.

The German citizens of the town of Dachau were later forced to bury the 9,000 dead inmates found at the camp.

Joe Johnson at Dachau

Our Hero Interviewee Joe Johnson had told me that he actually personally blew up one of the crematoriums at Dachau. I asked him to tell us about it.

JOE JOHNSON: Dachau. Yeah, here again the CIA was with us. They had requested General George Patton to provide part of his Third Army to go behind the lines in Dachau.

They told him that we have got to get Dachau. They gassed those Jews by the thousands up there, women and children everyday. We got to destroy it and do something to stop that killing, so Patton came down there and got all the fuel and ammunition for three days. We didn't know where we was going, he didn't tell us. We traveled all night and we got there the next morning.

We had American fighter planes over the top of us. We didn't know why they was there, we didn't know, but anyway when it come daylight real good and the CIA guy rolled a map out on the jeep, the hood of the jeep. He said this is Dachau. This is the four corners where the guards are where they are guarding them.

We don't have no way to take prisoners if they want to surrender. But if they fire at you then you can shoot back; you can kill them. So as soon as those German guards seen us we never seen them no more. The last thing I seen of them was their shoe soles going through the woods like a deer.

Dachau was a terrible thing so we carried TNT to disassemble that thing. We put TNT under that old incinerator back there where they had the gas chamber, where they had those people at and we destroyed that.

We put that TNT explosive and destroyed every bit of it. I seen that tin going up towards the moon, I don't know when it came down, but I know we destroyed it and got rid of it.

It was a great blessing to do that. We had the privilege to go in that camp and see what was in there after we done that.

***

General Eisenhower was keenly aware of the need for eyewitness accounts to preserve for history the horrors of the camps. He described his visit to Ohrdruf concentration camp to General George Marshall:

"The visual evidence and the verbal testimony of starvation, cruelty and bestiality were so overpowering as

244

to leave me a bit sick. In one room, where they were piled up twenty or thirty naked men, killed by starvation, George Patton would not even enter. He said that he would get sick if he did so.

I made the visit deliberately, in order to be in a position to give first-hand evidence of these things if ever, in the future, there develops a tendency to charge these allegations merely to 'propaganda'.

While General George S. Patton would not go in the room stacked with bodies, he did see bodies stacked about the camp. He wrote in his diary:

"There was a pile of about 40 completely naked human bodies in the last stages of emaciation. These bodies were lightly sprinkled with lime, not for the purposes of destroying them, but for the purpose of removing the stench."

***

In addition to the camps per se, Hitler took many other escalating actions against the Jews.

The entire world watched as Hitler caused the "Nuremberg Laws" to be passed September 15, 1935. These Laws deprived Jews of German citizenship, removed Jews from all spheres of German political, social and economic life, and established definitions of what a Jew is and created severe discrimination against people who even had a Jewish grandparent.

Hitler opened the Buchenwald concentration camp July 15, 1937.

He passed a law requiring Jews to register their property April 26, 1938.

Hitler was encouraged that the world viewed him and his Jewish policies favorably by three events:

1. January 2, 1939 Time Magazine names him Man of the Year;

2. May 17, 1939 the British issue the Palestine "White Paper" fixing the upper limit of Jews allowed to be admitted into Palestine over the next five years to 75,000;

3. June 1939 the rejection of the steamship carrying 937 Jewish refugees fleeing Hamburg is turned away by every country, including the United States. Even though they were eventually split up and taken in by England, Holland, France and Belgium, the rejections and the eventual limited acceptances tells Hitler that the nations of the world seem to support his theory of the Jews; or at least the world is unconcerned with the plight of the Jew.

Hitler felt he was on the right track.

Most of the world just watched and did nothing throughout all of these actions.

England and France continued to watch without doing anything until Hitler invaded Poland, forcing them to act. He invaded Poland September 1, 1939.

Hitler established the Auschwitz Concentration Camp May 20, 1940.

We in the United States just watched and did nothing until Hitler's allies, the Japanese, bombed our Pearl Harbor.

This was 16 years of doing nothing to stop him.

His horrors showed us the extreme of mankind's potential for cruelty, and left us with the most indelible of memories for World War II.

Chapter 6

Statistics

Russia made a tremendous sacrifice for the war effort.

Statistics vary but Soviet Union military casualties totaled at least 35 million, with approximately 14.7 million killed, missing or captured. Soviet civilian death toll probably reached 20 million. One in four Soviets was killed or wounded. Some 1,710 towns and 70,000 villages were destroyed.

These statistics are believed to be true, however the "official statistics" are somewhat lower as depicted in the chart for all participants.

Country	Military	Civilian	Total
USSR	12 million	17 million	29 million
Poland	597,000	5.86 million	6.27 million
Germany	3.25 million	2.44 million	5.69 million
Yugoslavia	305,000	1.35 million	1.66 million
Romania	450,000	465,000	915,000
Hungary	200,000	600,000	800,000
France	245,000	350,000	595,000
Italy	380,000	153,000	533,000
Great Britain	403,000	92,700	495,000
United States	407,000	6,000	413,000
Czechoslovakia	7,000	315,000	322,000
Holland	13,700	236,000	249,000
Greece	19,000	140,000	159,000
Belgium	76,000	23,000	99,000

These data tell us that in the countries listed, World War II resulted in the deaths of over 47 million people.

Other data as depicted in the chart below tell us that overall deaths were much higher.

World War II Statistics	
Number of Americans who served in World War II	16.1 million
Average amount of time each U.S. military serviceman served overseas during WWII	16 months
Number of people worldwide who served in WWII	1.9 billion
Number of deaths sustained worldwide during WWII	72 million
Number of European Jews killed during the holocaust	6 million
Number of U.S. troops engaged during WWII	16,112,566
Number of American casualties during WWII	291,557
Number of German Generals executed by Hitler	84
Number of bombs the allies dropped during WWII	3.4 million tons
Number of U.S. soldiers that were wounded during WWII	671,846
Number of men who served on U-Boats	40,000
Number of men who served on U-Boats who never returned	30,000
Number of German planes that were destroyed on accidents	45%
Number of airplanes that US 8th Air Force shot down	6,098
Total average amount of bombs dropped by the allies each month during WWII	27,770 tons
Number of countries involved in WWII	61 countries

About the Author John Long

I was born in a small three room house out in the country Northwest of Saltillo Mississippi in 1936. As a direct decent of an Irish immigrant, I grew up in an area known as "Barrett Ridge" which was named after my great Grandfather, Ned Barrett.

After high school, I joined the Army and was assigned to Heavy Mortar Company, 87th Infantry Regiment, 10th Infantry Division, spending almost two and a half years in Germany.

I then went to college in Memphis Tennessee and obtained two degrees from the University of Memphis, one being a law degree in 1965.

In 1967, I was elected county prosecuting attorney for Tupelo, Lee County, Mississippi and served four years.

Afterwards I practiced law in Lee County until I retired in 1994. Most of my practice included trying cases in front of a jury. I still maintain an active license to help people pro bono when I feel needed.

My life long friend, Walter Parks, an author and publisher is working with me to write this book because of my desire to preserve the memories of the last eyewitnesses from Normandy in World War II.

While many books have been written over the years about the war, we wanted this book to be a little different. I wanted these ordinary men with extraordinary courage to be heard and preserved for future generations.

Since my time in the Army my wife and I have been back to Germany many times; but we never visited the beaches of Normandy.

After watching a documentary about the paratroopers that dropped way off their jump zone and landed in a swamp below the little village of Graignes, France; my wife Helen and I decided to go to the D-Day Anniversary in Europe in 2013.

We went to Graignes and the beaches of Normandy. While there we began to lay the foundation for this book.

We stood on the beaches of the invasion and walked in the cemetery where so many soldiers made the ultimate sacrifice.

When we returned home we sought out surviving soldiers who fought in WWII.

It has been an incredible journey as my wife and I interviewed these gentlemen and listened to their stories.

We must preserve these last eyewitnesses' memories.

About the Author Walter Parks

Hi! Thanks so much for your interest in my books!

My principal interests are true stories of the unusual or of the previously Unknown or unexplained. I have occasionally also written some fiction.

I wrote this book with my life-long friend John Long because of his intense interest in recording the last memories of common but exceptional soldiers in World War II.

I was born in Memphis Tennessee and grew up in Saltillo Mississippi with John Long. Saltillo is a small town near Tupelo Mississippi.

High School life was dominated by watching the rise of our local Elvis. I was editor of the High School Paper and had plenty to write about. I guess this was the beginning of my writing career.

After graduating from Mississippi State University as an aerospace engineer I moved to Orlando Florida and worked for Lockheed Martin for 24 years. I advanced from an aerospace engineer to a Vice President of the Company and President of the Tactical Weapons Systems Division.

Education Activities

I continued my education throughout my career with a MBA degree from Rollins College and with Post Graduate Studies in Astrophysics at UCLA; Laser Physics at the University of Michigan; Computer Science at the University of Miami; Gas Dynamics at MMC and Finance and Accounting at the Wharton School, University of Pennsylvania.

While at Mississippi State University I was on the President's Honor List and in the honor societies of Tau Beta Pi, Sigma Gamma Tau and Blue Key.

I received a scholarship from Delta Air Lines based on my academics and performance.

I was in ROTC and the Arnold Air Society where I participated and toured as a member of the precision Drill Team. I also attended the summer survival training at Hamilton Air Force Base in California.

I was selected for Who's Who among Students in American Universities and Colleges.

I was a speaker for several technical organizations including the American Institute of Aeronautics and Astronautics.

After Retirement

After retirement from Lockheed I formed Parks-Jaggers Aerospace Company and sold it 4 years later.

After selling my aerospace company I formed Quest Studios, Quest Entertainment and Rosebud Entertainment to make films at Universal Studios. I produced 10 films, directed 7 films and wrote 5 film scripts produced at Universal Studios.

I won the National Association of Theater Owners Show South Producer of Tomorrow Award.

I then formed UnknownTruths Publishing Company to publish true stories of the unusual or of the previously Unknown or unexplained. These include books about past events so unbelievable that most people have relegated them to "myths".

I have published 33 books with 30 in eBook format, 25 in Paperback format and 28 as Audio Books.

I have an additional 12 books in development.

About Publishing Company

UnKnownTruths Publishing Company was formed to publish true stories of the unusual or of the previously Unknown or unexplained. These stories typically provide radically different views from those that have shaped the understandings of our natural world, our religions, our science, our history, and even the foundations of our civilizations.

The Company's stories also include stories of the very important anti-aging, life-extending medical breakthroughs; stem cell therapies; genetic therapies; cloning and other emerging findings that promise to change the very meaning of life.

The Company also publishes stories from the past that are so unbelievable that they are generally considered to be myths. The published stories provide the evidence for the truth.

The Company has published 35 books with 30 in eBook format, 27 in Paperback format and 28 as Audio Books.

UnknownTruths.com

info@UnknownTruths.com

Made in the USA
Middletown, DE
26 November 2020